DISCOVERING YOUR PAST LIVES

D1472471

CLASSICS OF PERSONAL DEVELOPMENT

DISCOVERING YOUR PAST LIVES

Spiritual growth through a knowledge of past lifetimes

Glenn Williston and Judith Johnstone

Thorsons
An Imprint of HarperCollinsPublishers

Thorsons
An Imprint of HarperCollins*Publishers*
77–85 Fulham Palace Road,
Hammersmith, London W6 8JB

First published as *Soul Search* 1983
Published by Aquarian 1988
This edition 1995
3 5 7 9 10 8 6 4 2

A catalogue record for this book
is available from the British Library

ISBN 1 85030 729 5

Printed and bound in Great Britain by
Caledonian International Book Manufacturing Ltd, Glasgow

CONTENTS

They know me not
who think that I am
   only flesh and blood –
   a transient dweller
   on the fragile spaceship earth
   that gave me birth.
For I am Spirit
   eternal, indestructible, not confined to space or time
   and when my sojourn here is through
   my roles fulfilled, my assignments done
   I will lay aside this space suit called my body
   and move on to other mansions, roles, assignments
   in our Father's house of eternal life.
   So dry your tears
   weep not overmuch for me – or for yourself.
   Set me free
   in the Love that holds us all
   and makes us one eternally!
   Our paths will cross again
   Our minds and hearts will touch
   Our souls will shout with joy and laughter
   As we recall
   the lives we've lived
   the worlds we've seen
   the ways we've trod
   to find ourselves – at last –
     in God.

J. SIG PAULSON, *ETERNAL VISION*

PREFACE

When we wrote the first edition of this book in the early 1980s, neither of us could have imagined the wonderful response it would evoke. From all over the world readers have written to share their experiences, ask questions, and thank us for bringing a new and healing perspective into their lives. But there was one question that recurred time and again. Why was the book written in first person singular when there were two authors' names on the cover? When more than one reader made the assumption that the second 'author' was a disincarnate spirit, it began to seem important that we set the record straight.

We made the decision to use the first person because much of *Discovering Your Past Lives* is a record of Glenn Williston's pioneering work in the use of past life regressions as a therapeutic tool. While still living in New England, Dr Williston had begun these explorations with clients who came to him for psychological therapy. When he decided to relocate his home and practice in California, the dream of transforming his records and transcriptions into a book was necessarily deferred.

Judith Johnstone, a writer and editor whose career was in book publishing, met Glenn Williston shortly after he arrived on the West Coast. In time it became clear that the way to get the story told was by collaboration. *Discovering Your Past Lives* expanded during the writing process to include a chapter giving historical perspective and other chapters of a spiritual nature. During the entire process of writing, Judith Johnstone was – and remains – an earthly being.

Both authors are intensely grateful for the privilege of bringing healing information to readers seeking knowledge and comfort as all of us move along the path of spiritual awakening.

Glenn Williston, Ph.D.

Judith Johnstone

PRISONERS OF THE PAST

≈

Into my heart an air that kills
  From yon far country blows;
What are those blue remembered hills,
  What spires, what farms are those?

That is the land of lost content,
  I see it shining plain,
The happy highways where I went
  And cannot come again.

A. E. HOUSMAN, *A SHROPSHIRE LAD*

Within each eternal Soul reside the memories and perceptions of many lifetimes. Meticulously recorded, these images play an important role in shaping the persons we are today. Just as a child's earliest experiences have a profound influence on the later adult, so the stored knowledge of past lives contributes to and affects our present choices and decisions. This contribution may be generally positive or negative, depending entirely upon the character of those past events and the way in which we handled them.

Some people find that this lifetime is unfolding in a way that is reasonably satisfying and rewarding, and they feel no need to delve into the early events of this life – or those that preceded it (though some will choose to do so simply out of curiosity – that very human desire to *know*). But for others, try as they will, the satisfactions of life always seem to elude them and they feel powerless to deal with dimly perceived imperatives that mysteriously rule their lives.

In some cases it is necessary to recall certain scenes of childhood in order to reach the source of the negative beliefs that are wreaking havoc in the life of the adult, but in many others the primal event occurred in a past life and it can never be completely resolved without recalling and re-experiencing the feelings that accompanied it. Fortunately, we are now able to do this through a combination of traditional therapeutic techniques and hypnotic past-life regressions. The cases that follow show the results of such an approach.

*   *   *   *   *   *

'Something terrible is going to happen to me on a boat', said Janet, 'and I am deathly afraid of deep water.' The thirty-year-old teacher had lived by the ocean all her life, yet she perched tensely in the reclining chair as she told me how her fears had prevented her from sharing the pleasures of sailing and swimming with her friends. Her father was a fisherman, her mother was an avid swimmer, and her brothers and sisters had no fear of water. Nothing in her conscious memory revealed any incident in her childhood that would account for such fear.

As I spoke quietly to her, Janet's body settled into the big chair, her breathing softened, and her skin took on the waxy appearance that is characteristic of deep hypnosis. Together we began the journey back in time through her childhood, her birth experience, and into her pre-natal existence. Nothing significant came to light. Then slowly a scene began to unfold that took place before Janet's birth, even before her womb experience. We had gone back to an earlier life.

Her name was no longer Janet, it was Mary. Mary Janette Brouley. The place was no longer a small town in Rhode Island; we were transported to the English countryside. The voice I listened to changed from the Eastern accent of a mature woman to the soft British tones of a young girl. The time was 1894. The girl Mary described a scene where horses clip-clopped over packed dirt roads and cobblestone streets, and fishermen hummed sea shanties as they repaired their nets on the stone wall at the water's edge.

Mary's mother was dying. Having attended to her mother's needs for several days, Mary decided that she needed a breath of fresh air. Walking alone by the wharf, she was suddenly startled by a flash of light from the water and, moments later, a terrible crashing sound. Mary gasped as she began to describe for me the collision of two ships.

'Out in the water . . . a terrible crash. People screaming, screaming. Mostly the sound of men's voices. The fire . . . the flames and the fire! I can see them from the shore. The sky is lit by the flames from the boats. All the people are in the water . . . all in the water. Oh, the crash . . . people running to the waterfront to see. The noise and screaming and nobody can do anything.

'Everyone died. Not one person lived. It was November and the water was icy. Sir William, the schoolmaster, was on one of those boats. The fisherman loved him, he was so kind.' [Mary broke into sobs.] He never came back, he never came back. So many people I knew. My brother John Martin was on one of the boats. He left four children. They built a monument for the men . . . to the disaster. November 1894. It is just outside Matthew Bridgeton's fish shop. They were all from the village, and they left little ones. Oh, they left so many little ones. Herbert Swain and the brother James . . . so many names on the spire.'

It was clear now that Janet, as Mary Brouley, had witnessed a terrible disaster and felt the panic and helplessness of death by fire and drowning even though she was only an observer. She may have been rendered more susceptible to the emotions of the scene because of her deep concern for her dying mother, though the loss of her brother and many other close friends was reason enough for a lasting impression. It took four more sessions during which Janet confronted that terrifying scene before she was able to discharge all the emotions connected with it. At that point she was released from her fear of deep water and the notion that something dreadful would happen to her in a boat.

* * * * * *

Helen should by now have recovered from the shock of her husband's death two years earlier. She needed the companionship of friends and relatives, but instead of sending herself back into the mainstream of life, Helen was retreating further and further into a world of isolation and loneliness. She had loved her husband very much and his unexpected death from a heart attack was a great loss, but her withdrawal from the world, intensifying with each passing month, did not appear justified. Yet she was seemingly powerless to turn things around. We decided to explore long-forgotten memories to see if a clue could be found.

Helen regressed quite easily to a scene in her childhood in which her father abandoned the family. I had hoped that we could explore even earlier memories than the one she presented, but Helen did not believe in reincarnation. This I accepted, although successful past-life regressions do not depend on one's belief in the validity of reincarnation. At the end of the session Helen said she felt some measure of relief from having contacted that scene of rejection by her father. We both hoped this would break her out of her prison of fear and allow her to resume an active life.

I did not hear from Helen for nearly a week. Then late one night she telephoned, waking me from a dream about a murder. 'I am going to kill myself. I have a gun aimed at my temple and my finger is on the trigger,' she said. 'There is no use going on. I still feel trapped. I have no freedom. What's the use?' Groggy, not sure what was dream and what was reality, I let her talk. Finally I suggested that she wait to take her life until after coming in for an early morning session. She agreed.

Seven in the morning is early to see anyone, let alone a suicidal client, but I was ready when Helen arrived at 6:55. Her first words were that her gun was in the purse which she clutched to her body. Progress, I thought. At least her finger was not on the trigger.

Without any preliminary discussion, I asked Helen to seat herself comfortably and begin relaxing her body, which she did with great difficulty. Tears came to her closed eyes several times during the induction process. I reassured her that we would not be concerned with a deep state of hypnosis, just as much relaxation as she could allow. I asked her to let her mind drift and to 'play along with me'. This is a phrase I often use with reluctant clients because it tends to reduce effort and self-consciousness. 'We are going back in time', I told her, assuming a rhythmical speech pattern and softer tone. 'We are going back in time and space and you are freeing your mind to drift. Go as far back as you . . .'. Helen interrupted me.

'The sun is warm and Daddy has allowed us to have the party on the lawn. The sky is so blue and everyone is so happy. Daddy has brought me a silver mirror set and I had Addie put it on my dresser. I'm going to show it to the others after the party.'

Gone were the tears. Now Helen smiled broadly as she described her sprawling plantation home outside Atlanta in 1855. I asked questions to encourage her to experience everything as fully as possible. Helen, as Nora Mae, was celebrating her sixteenth birthday. She spoke lovingly of her father and of the close bond she had with her nanny, Addie.

Nora Mae loved riding Jaunty, her favourite horse, at a wild gallop though the fields and nearby woods, feeling the wind in her face and the sense of trust and freedom that comes with riding a horse. Many of her descriptive phrases mentioned or implied freedom and love of life, along with great involvement in activities with her friends. No traumatic scenes emerged during the reconstruction of the entire lifetime of Nora Mae. Even her death was peaceful at the age of ninety-two.

Helen opened her eyes on the count of zero, but she seemed to be looking through me rather than at me. She smiled delightedly and exclaimed 'What a glorious life that was!' Together we reviewed the highlights of her life as Nora Mae and I had never seen Helen so animated.

That evening I received another phone call from Helen. Much to my surprise, she was not calling from her home; she was calling from a phone booth to report that she was stranded without money or gasoline. Exhilarated, Helen recountered the events of her day, which began with a shopping spree in the morning, included a visit to her daughter in the afternoon, and ended with her going to the movies. 'But I didn't watch my pennies', she said, 'and now I'm stranded.' Going to her rescue, I reflected happily on the contrast to our earlier meeting. Helen was free.

Helen's case, like a number of others, was interesting because it was not necessary to discover the primal event from the past that was triggering the present crisis. Though I feel certain that such an event existed, Helen's re-experiencing a former life filled with freedom and self-expression was enough to nullify present fears and allow her to resume her active life.

*　*　*　*　*　*

The pretty blonde teenager who sat before me was timid and self-conscious as she told me about her compelling, almost obsessive, need to help both animals and people in distress. Jean related a truly impressive series of incidents going back into her childhood that involved rescuing stray dogs, repairing broken bird wings, and shoring up various humans who came to depend on her. Despite this, Jean seemed to have no confidence in herself. She came to me for career counselling and for help in understanding her motivations in playing the rescuer to one and all.

At first, it appeared that simple vocational counselling might help her to focus her latent abilities and channel her need to help others. This, combined with sessions of hypnosis to improve her self-image and her communication skills would probably be adequate to launch Jean on the road to a happy life. However, Jean mentioned that her grandmother's experience of several past lives through self-hypnosis had made Jean curious about the influence in her own life of possible former lives. She wanted to try a regression.

Jean, it turned out, was one of a small percentage of subjects (10 to 15 per cent) who go into a deep stage of hypnosis very quickly in response to a few well-chosen words. Usually a person who inducts this quickly has no recall of the experience on a conscious level, and this was the case with Jean – afterwards she apologized for falling asleep and wasting my time!

'The hands of the clock are spinning backwards', I said slowly, allowing her to visualize the clock. 'You will find you are some-where, doing something, at the count of five. One, two, three, four, five.' Jean opened her eyes widely and, just as I was about to suggest that she close them so we could try again, I realized that she was focused on another time and place and was totally oblivious to the office where her physical body lay motionless. I made my usual pronouncement about understanding English and responding in English to facilitate communications; she could feel free, however, to use expressions of another language and would be able to recall them later if asked to do so.

Jean said nothing. Instead, she raised her finger and began to form some kind of symbols in the air. At first, I could make no sense of any of the symbols, one of which looked something like a snake. As she repeated the symbols, it clicked; the snake was a backward S. I grabbed my pen to record the backwards letters, then rummaged through my desk for a mirror. The mirror revealed what she had written. BOSTON.

'Don't you wish to speak?', I asked Jean. Her only response was to point to her throat. Intriguing as this was, I suspected that the regression would have to be shortened because of our difficulty in communicating. Then I had an idea.

'Go ahead twenty years in that lifetime', I said. 'Yes', came the slow, soft reply. She relaxed her hand in her lap and closed her eyes.

'Do you have any physical impairment?'

'I have just recently learned to talk. Johnn (she spelled his name with two ens) has taught me. He is so wonderfully patient. I am blind and deaf and could not speak in words until five years ago. I am twenty-nine now. We came to live in Boston when I was eight. My father took me out of the wagon and traced the letters of the "Boston" sign with my fingers as we were entering the city. I will never forget it. It was the first thing I thought of when I learned about words.'

Here was a memory within a memory. Jean, as Sara Thomas, went on to describe in great detail the muddy streets of nineteenth-century Boston and the furnishings of the comfortable home in which she lived with her husband-tutor, Johnn. She spoke of her family, but most of all about learning to communicate.

When she had finished her story, I turned Jean's attention to choosing an occupation that would suit her in this lifetime.

'Physical therapy would be a sound choice', she said with no hesitation. 'I understand living with limitations'.

A much more confident Jean emerged from this session. The last I heard from her, she had finished her training in physical rehabilitation and was enthusiastically launching her career.

* * * * * *

Many alcoholics seek to control their desire for alcohol through hypnosis. However, because of their difficulty in concentrating (the most important factor in the induction process), most of them are disappointed with the results obtained through hypnosis alone. Intensive group and individual counselling along with a carefully formulated nutritional programme are usually more successful for the strongly motivated alcoholic. Because of this, I only reluctantly agreed when Josh's father implored me to see his son.

Josh arrived twenty minutes late for his appointment. He appeared to be about forty years old and his body clearly indicated the ravages of alcohol. It was bloated and the skin was thin, almost translucent, and prematurely wrinkled. He trembled constantly and dropped the pen twice as he filled out the information card, which gave his age as twenty-six.

Tears rolled freely down his cheeks from the moment Josh began to speak. His extreme sensitivity and frustration were readily apparent as he told how the divorce of his parents had changed his life. He seldom saw his mother because she had moved to the East Coast. Josh had no women friends and had great difficulty even finding a date. Everything was just too much effort. His employer had been understanding at first, but now his patience was running out.

Josh had just one question for me: WHY? I told him we would try to find out. Our first attempt at hypnosis was unsuccessful. The next three sessions were also unfruitful, though Josh faithfully complied with my request that he should not drink for at least six hours beforehand. Finally he developed enough trust in me and in the hypnotic process so that he was able to relax and focus his attention sufficiently to experience a past-life regression. My voice was his guide through a long dark tunnel with a light at the end where a scene would unfold.

'It seems to be a field with something planted', Josh said slowly as he tried to focus. Then, quite unexpectedly, 'I hate them! I hate them! I hate everyone of the bloodthirsty savages!'.

'Indians?', I asked.

'White men are savages. I am an Indian . . . a Blackfoot', Josh corrected me with dignity.

He slipped more and more into his life as a Blackfoot. His speech became the clipped words of the Indian who learned English as a second language. His physical features changed before my eyes. (This happens in nearly 25 per cent of all regressions). 'Go back slightly in time', I instructed him, for Josh was describing his hatred for the white man without hitting upon the incident that triggered the feelings.

'Three of them . . . with guns, on horses . . . riding through my corn. My wife . . . great with child . . . picking corn. Yelling and screaming . . . they were drunk. I called to my Little Bird Song but it was too late. They trampled the corn . . . and my wife and the child in her body. They didn't even care . . . laughed and threw corn at me. I wanted to kill them. I will get back at them. They killed my wife, and the child who had not seen the light of one day, the halo of one full moon. I will sneak into the town at night and kill them all.'

Josh as the Blackfoot Indian did not live long enough to follow through with his resolve, for two days later he contracted a fever and died. That negative energy remained with him, however – he still had a self-destructive need for revenge.

Josh was aware of everything he said during the regression, as most subjects are, and he saw at once that he had answered his own question. Now he knew why he drank so obsessively. Two days after this session, Josh called to say that he had taken a leave of absence from his job and entered a centre for the treatment of alcoholism 'to change my life around'. Having previously refused to attend even one Alcoholics Anonymous meeting, Josh now traded the nebulous world of the bottle for the clinical regimentation of the hospital. At last he had a fighting chance for success.

*   *   *   *   *   *

Linda was terrified whenever the ball came toward her in gym class. She could not bring herself to catch a ball, nor could she return one in sports like badminton or tennis. Though she told herself that it was foolish, the fourteen-year-old was so afraid of flying objects that she was unable to participate in the physical education programme. School officials were sympathetic, but they suggested that Linda's parents seek counselling for their otherwise healthy daughter.

Linda was a good subject from the start. Easily a scene unfolded.

'There are trees and a river and I'm very afraid. There are people coming. I'm alone. They can see me in my long, blue dress. The people are after me. They think I did something wrong and they are out to get me. No, no, no. [She began to sob] I'm so afraid'.

Linda was trembling as she identified with the feelings of that past-life experience.

'Go back in time', I suggested, 'so that we can find out what they think you did'. Linda took a moment to allow the scene to become clear.

'I'm in a courtroom, standing in front of a judge. I can hardly stand . . . I feel sick and my knees are buckling under me. I have been accused of witchcraft. He is pointing at me and pronouncing the sentence. "Thee, Elizabeth Bradley, having been accused and proven guilty of the abominable deed of witchcraft, shall be hanged by the neck until dead".'

'But I'm not a witch!' Linda's sobbing increased.

'The woman hates me. I never did anything to her but she's jealous. I'm young and pretty and John is handsome. She's old and she thinks I have everything. I've never hurt her in any way. I have no relatives to defend me. John is afraid to do anything. I've got to get away, got to get away!

'I dashed out of the courthouse and I ran as fast as I could. My lungs hurt, my legs were numb. My mind spun in circles. I didn't know where I was going, but I knew I had to get away.

'But they are coming after me . . . it's a mob . . . some women, but mostly men.' [Linda is now sobbing loudly and shaking visibly] 'They are picking up stones and throwing them at me. They are throwing stones at me, all of them. [There is surprise in her voice.] I can't run any farther. I am at the edge of the lake. I can't get away and they are getting closer. I can't get away . . . all sizes of stones. They are hitting me with them . . .' [Silence now.]

'Tell me more', I urged. 'What has happened?' Elizabeth Bradley finally spoke in a soft whisper.

'A large stone hits me in the head. The pain is horrible. I fall down and die instantly. I gave up trying to get away. I had no choice. Now I am free, free, free.

'I can see my body. I am looking down on my body. The mob is standing over it. One man turns me over with his foot and mumbles something to the others. They are going to take it away. I don't want to stay with my body anymore. I am free. And light . . . I love the light, peaceful feeling . . . no more fear and pain. I am free.'

The sense of freedom that Linda experienced after being stoned to death as Elizabeth now carried over into her conscious mind in this present life. She no longer feared flying objects, and her beginner's enthusiasm in sports earned her an A in physical education the next term.

*   *   *   *   *   *

Past-life regression is an important therapeutic tool, and in my experience several thousand clients have relived one or more past lives. They have benefited in a multitude of ways – gaining greater self-knowledge, a release from guilt, a release from the fear of death, an increased sense of hope and freedom, a deeper understanding of the Soul, and a stronger sense of kinship with all human beings. Vexatious personal problems such as those in the preceding cases, are often ameliorated or dissolved through explorations of past lives.

The past-life regression is a means of getting to those traumas that have occurred to a person in a former life and continue to wreak havoc in the present. The regression may be accompanied by great emotion, even pain, yet this confrontation is always worth whatever trauma is experienced. There are few miracle cures here. While some people immediately let go of abnormal fear or anxiety after re-experiencing a past-life trauma, the usual course is that greater knowledge and understanding of the material in the unconscious leads gradually and inevitably to a more satisfying life.

The exploration of past lives is, of course, based upon the concept of reincarnation, where the Soul is born into a succession of lives in the physical world in order to encounter growth opportunities in the progression towards total maturity. Because I have seen the practical ramifications of reincarnation in my daily work for so many years, I no longer have the slightest doubt as to its validity. There was a time, however, when I felt differently.

CONFRONTATION WITH MYSELF

≈

> *The longest journey*
> *Is the journey inwards*
> *Of him who has chosen his destiny,*
> *Who has started upon his quest*
> *For the source of his being . . .*
>
> DAG HAMMARSKJOLD, *MARKINGS*

Lines from Shelley, Keats and Wordsworth swirled through my head as I indulged in that peculiarly clandestine pleasure of feeling sorry for myself. Every day I drove the length of the state of Rhode Island to attend classes which left me feeling pessimistic about the future of public education in the United States and about my own future as well. I was holding down a monotonous job in order to pay my own way as I studied to become a teacher, yet teaching seemed less and less attractive as I plodded through the stultifying education courses required for certification.

Feelings of helplessness overwhelmed me. Teaching had always appealed to me because of my strong desire to help others, but from this new perspective it seemed to offer very little of value to anyone. Seeing myself as a pawn in the meaningless game of life (the phrase 'victim of Fate' appealed to me), I spent many hours brooding over the English Romantic and Victorian poets. In more realistic moments I saw clearly that I could hardly hope to serve others when I could not even help myself; perhaps I should see a counsellor. But then I fell back on the excuse that the student poverty which I so much resented made counselling impossible. Certainly taking on another job was out of the question.

I was confused, bored, frustrated, and depressed. I was also firmly atheistic. Having rejected my middle-of-the-road Protestant religious training, I also summarily dismissed any notion of a conscious universe or a Divine Order. I resolved to believe only in that which could be seen and felt; this seemed a realistic and scientific point of view.

To my astonishment, several of my college friends believed in reincarnation. They often talked about having lived other lives. I was torn between laughing at them and trying to disabuse them of their delusions. If Protestant Christianity had provided nothing for me, the idea of struggling through one meaningless life after another was even less appealing. In fact, it sent chills up and down my spine. Often these discussions about other lifetimes left me even more depressed than before.

Late one evening a fellow sufferer in my poetry class boldly presented the statement that William Blake believed in reincarnation. Neatly typed on a piece of thesis paper were these lines from *Visions of the Daughters of Albion*:

Tell me where dwell the thoughts forgotten till thou call them forth?
Tell me where dwell the joys of old? and where the ancient loves,
And when they will renew again, and the night of oblivion past,
That I might traverse times and spaces far remote, and bring
Comforts into a present sorrow and a night of pain?

I thought I detected a conspiracy when the following day another friend, obviously in league with the Blake expert, shifted the lunchtime conversation to a tedious listing of famous proponents of reincarnation. I heard of Bronson Alcott, Alexander the Great, Balzac, Beethoven, and Elizabeth Barrett Browning before excusing myself to return my tray to the kitchen. As I re-entered the dining room to pick up my books, John was just getting to the T's. What a bore!

Much to my annoyance, the next few days found me preoccupied with the absurdity of reincarnation. One evening I sat down and made a list of all the arguments I could think of that countered the idea. I could excuse my feeble-minded friends' belief in reincarnation because it was the 'in' thing. How such great minds as Plato, Emerson, Hegel and Tolstoy could embrace the theory was simply beyond me.

Awakening to the limpid air of a perfect April morning, I was especially restless and decided to skip the usual routine. Providence is a nice city in which to stroll (especially when one is avoiding responsibility or fighting off insights from higher levels of being!). Choosing side streets lined with small shops, I scarcely noticed where I was. My feet seemed to know where I was going, even though my brain did not. Shortly before noon I found myself standing outside a bookstore. Accustomed to being chronically short of money, I had a personal rule that I would not enter a bookstore unless I could afford to buy a book. Since there were only a couple of dollars in my pocket, I began to retreat.

Before I knew what I was doing, I was inside the store and standing before the section labelled METAPHYSICS, OCCULT, RELIGION. This was the last place I wanted to be! My hand reached out and took from the shelf a green paperback I felt I *had* to have. The back cover copy was nonsense, I told myself, yet I was intrigued, and the first few pages of the book got me hooked. At the counter I dug into my pockets to find every cent I had with me, and a thorough search yielded $2.04, which happened to be the exact price of the book. A crazy idea raced though my mind that, in a full-fledged conspiracy, my friends had planted the book and then somehow lured me into the store. By whatever means, the book was mine. That night, long after everyone else had gone to bed, I devoured *The Search for Bridey Murphy*.

So captivated was I by the story of Ruth Simmons' regression by hypnosis to her former life as the nineteenth-century Irish woman Bridey Murphy that within a few days I had located phonograph records of the taped sessions that formed the basis of the book. The

Irish brogue of the spirited young lass was in marked contrast to the flat midwestern accent of Wisconsin-born Ruth Simmons. Bridey's attitudes and opinions, her recollection of many obscure details of life in Cork and Belfast a century ago, and the logical order of events that could be reconstructed from the random memories she recounted all offered persuasive evidence to me – the quintessential sceptic – that Mrs Simmons had actually been recalling a past life.

A profound transition began to take place within me as I searched out and read everything I could find on the subjects of reincarnation and hypnosis. Gradually I gave up the idea of myself as the helpless victim of a blind universe. I came to understand that there is a vastly complex Consciousness in which we all operate, governed by the laws of cause and effect, and that we are entirely responsible for the substance and direction of our own lives.

During this period of my life I finished my degree and began teaching. Having enough of psychology and education courses, I looked for wisdom about human nature in literature and earned a Master's degree in that field. In addition to teaching studies, I trained teachers in the classroom. But the aspect of my work that was most important to me from the beginning was counselling, and over the intervening years it increasingly occupied my time. The educator in me is now expressed through lectures, seminars, and writing.

In 1977 I established Soul Search Foundation, later to become Alternative Therapies Council, an organization devoted to the understanding of people as multi-dimensional beings who vibrate on frequencies of Body, Mind, Soul, and Spirit. This holistic view of human beings is the guiding principle for the Council's various educational programmes.

Past-life counselling is the best-known aspect of the Council's work. In each life we accumulate both good and bad experiences that continue to influence us years and even centuries later. By relaxing our minds we are able to return to those times of negative influence and rid ourselves of their control over the present. Hypnotic regression is the most direct method for doing this.

I have shared in the joys and sorrows of several thousand past (and future!) lives. To witness a person assume a different personality, speak with a different intonation and inflection, utter obscure or archaic colloquial expressions, and even converse in a foreign language unknown to them in this lifetime, is to accept the validity of reincarnation. To watch the expressions of a disbeliever listening to a taped regression or witnessing one in person is an experience matched only by a personal confrontation with another lifetime. Now, eighteen years after my precipitous collision with Bridey Murphy, I can state without any reservation that we have all experienced many lives, in many bodies, in many diverse places, and under a variety of circumstances – all along the continuum of Soul growth.

It is not the purpose of this book to make converts, but to cultivate a sense of awareness, a sense of power that comes from the spiritual freedom that is the birthright of every one of us. As we come to understand universal laws more fully it is clear that each of us is a part of a marvellously integrated system that nurtures us as we express our own lively individuality. The better we understand our relationship with the universe, the more we can free ourselves to be the magnificent persons we are destined to be.

Obviously I have no intention of taking some sort of 'objective' point of view. I believe without question in the existence of the Soul and in reincarnation. That we can remember other lifetimes through hypnosis as well as by other means has been demonstrated for me so persuasively thousands of times that any other explanation of the phenomenon is preposterous by comparison. Though the concept of reincarnation has been slow to take root in modern Western thought, it is an established tenet of faith for more than half the people of the world.

When people discover that I have used past-life regression as a counselling tool for many years, they are often curious about it. Usually they wonder what possible value there can be in exploring former lives, and sometimes they are fearful: perhaps they might unearth something that is better left buried. Addressing the question of fear, I point out that knowledge is strength, and any unrecognized traumas lurking in our subconscious minds serve to weaken us and keep us imprisoned as we try to deal with everyday life. 'Know the truth, and the truth shall make you free.' The Apostle John laid the cornerstone for all modern therapeutic technique with these words recorded in the New Testament.

One of the common and very welcome results of past-life regression is relief from the traumas of various kinds through remembering and reliving the primal events from which they have sprung. This reduction of stress is the primary benefit of such regressions. The cases cited in Chapter 1 illustrate this, yet they represent only a rather dramatic tip of the iceberg.

Perhaps one of the most profound responses to past-life regression is that inevitably it relieves the fear of death. Without exception, death is experienced in regression as a painless withdrawal from the final moment of life, the person usually lingering in spiritual form to observe the activity surrounding the body from which he or she has just departed. Many people fear that they will simply cease to exist when they die, and the memory of one or more death experiences where they remained fully conscious beings through the process of physical death – and beyond – is enormously reassuring.

For the many people who have pondered the mysteries of the Soul and dealt with the trauma of death, this book will come as no surprise. Dr Elizabeth Kübler-Ross [*On Death and Dying*] and Dr Raymond Moody [*Life after Life*] have made tremendous contributions to understanding the experience of death. The cases reported later in this book provide further evidence of a fully conscious, positive experience of death – an idea now accepted by a widening circle of professionals and lay people.

The re-experiencing of past lives can, and often does, lead to a greatly expanded view of the universe and our place within it. It puts us in touch with our Greater Selves [our Souls] and lends perspective on religious and spiritual matters.

Inferences drawn from exploring other lives lead us to recognize universal laws. It is possible to let go of fatalistic thinking after observing the law of cause and effect [karma] in operation *and correctly identifying oneself as the cause.* The view of human beings as energy sources rather than solid physical bodies helps us to understand spirituality on a scientific as well as a metaphysical level and leads to an understanding of the power of thoughts and emotions. The arbitrary nature of time is evident as its fluid and changeable aspects are revealed; this has the salutary effect of relieving the pressure of time which haunts and incapacitates so many of us.

The potentialities for self-development are virtually limitless, as the following list suggests. It would be absurd to contend that any one person is likely to expand in all of the areas mentioned, though there is no reason to suppose it impossible. Recalling and re-experiencing the dramas of past lives can help us to:

1. Reduce stress
2. Control or eliminate pain, guilt, anxiety, fears
3. Develop a sense of focus and concentration
4. Develop latent talents and unlock personal potentials
5. Ignite a sense of responsibility
6. Understand parents and other close associates
7. Relieve repressed emotions; release past hurts
8. Develop power, control, choice, confidence in all our actions
9. Avoid illness by recognizing earliest symptoms
10. Improve visualization, a key to self-healing
11. Reveal the meaning and purpose of life
12. Become beings of action rather than reaction

Exploring past lives through regression establishes an awareness of the uniqueness of each individual and at the same time affirms the brotherhood of all human beings. It makes nonsense of prejudice and shows that desire for retribution is meaningless. This clears the way for projecting and planning a much more meaningful and satisfying future.

Important as all these benefits can be, we cannot overlook curiosity as a significant motivation for wishing to know about the past. Curiosity sparks creativity and self-expression. It is natural for people to want answers to persistent questions about the meaning of life, as well as to the perplexities of their daily lives.

Henry Wadsworth Longfellow speaks of the universal longing for knowledge and mastery of the dimly perceived undercurrents in each of us:

So comes to us at times, from the unknown
And inaccessible solitudes of being,
The rushing of the sea-tides of the soul;
And inspirations, that we deem our own,
Are some divine foreshadowing and foreseeing
Of things beyond our reason or control.

Fortunately, it is no longer necessary to believe that parts of us are beyond our reason or control.

ANCIENT WISDOM

≈

Tell me not in mournful numbers,
Life is but an empty dream!
For the soul is dead that slumbers,
And things are not what they seem.
Life is real! Life is earnest!
And the grave is not its goal;
Dust thou art, to dust returnest,
Was not spoken of the soul.

HENRY WADSWORTH LONGFELLOW,
A PSALM OF LIFE

Reflecting on my student experience, I now see that while my conscious mind was trying to dismiss reincarnation as some sort of vague Eastern hocus-pocus, something more patient and indwelling was urging me to turn away from that stubborn position. It would be easier, I thought then, to believe what my religion had taught me – filled as it was with ambiguities and contradictions – than to consider a totally different system of belief, even if it was one embraced by more than a billion people. A philosophy that held me personally responsible for my actions and the events of my life certainly held no enchantment for me. Only after my curious encounter with Bridey Murphy was I able to lay aside my prejudices and fears sufficiently to understand and accept reincarnation.

Reincarnation is a very simple concept. It holds that human beings, like all other forms of nature, experience cycles of life, death, and rebirth which are subject to the laws of karma (cause and effect) and are evolutionary, leading ultimately to total unification with

≈ 21

God. The corollary of this belief is that each of us is personally responsible for our own actions and their consequences. While this concept may at first seem frightening, the truth is that a great sense of freedom grows out of the awareness that we are not pawns of fate, but rather that we are free to create precisely the lives we wish.

I had not long been a counsellor when it became clear that many other people faced the dilemma I had faced as a student. Their religion did not deal adequately with their deepest needs and yet they clung to it for its very familiarity. I have met many individuals who know about reincarnation either intuitively or experientially, but they hesitate to discuss it with family or friends because they perceive it to be in conflict with their religion. Some people are reluctant to enter into past-life exploration because of this.

A client named Jack once came to me because a religious 'war' was raging within him; one part of him strongly rejected his Protestant upbringing, yet another part of him was pre-occupied – almost obsessed – with religion. Jack was hoping to get at the roots of his dilemma, and he slipped quite readily into a deep hypnotic state. In an unfaltering stream of words and a casually conversational manner, Jack set the scene.

'We are in a study where I am studying a manuscript. I am Brother Timothy and this is the library of a monastery near Geneva, on the lake. I am wearing robes. Studying manuscripts is my work; we each have our duties. I happen to be a scholar of the early Christian Era'.

'What is the date today?', I interjected.

'Oh, this is April 18 1409. It's a Thursday', he said. Brother Timothy continued painting a portrait of his life and times.

'I took my name from Timothy, Paul's cousin. I confide my work in Brother James, who took his name from the brother of Jesus, and in Brother John. I feel like a neophyte compared to Brother John, since he has been studying in this area many more years than I. He says that some day these matters will be studied openly, without endangering communication in our Catholic faith. I know I am on the road to Truth, and if you know that, you cannot go wrong.'

When Jack paused for breath, I asked what were 'these matters' that 'endangered communication'. Immediately he adjusted his body to a more upright position in the reclining chair so that he appeared more official.

'You are not from Gregory, are you?', he asked quietly, his eyes still closed. Then, without waiting for a reply, 'No, of course you're not.' He smiled.

'Is Gregory a place or a person?', I asked.

'Pope Gregory', he replied. 'He would not approve at all'.

'Well [he went on], I have been very interested in Paul's travels, what he did just after his revelation, and what he and Timothy did to better organize a number of churches. Paul had a genuine vision of Christ, you know. [My ears pricked up].

'They were so close, I am certain there was a prior relationship between Paul and Jesus. Saul became a totally different personality after the vision, which is why he changed his name to Paul. That was what the vision was all about: CHRIST WAS REMINDING HIM OF THEIR EARLIER TIMES TOGETHER. I feel this will be common knowledge in the future, and many faiths will embrace this interpretation of the vision. Right now it is still dangerous to do so.'

Jack's regression to his life as Brother Timothy was intriguing. First, it provided many time-place references which we were later able to verify. Second, the scholar's conclusion that Saul's conversation on the road to Damascus came about because he had a revelation of a past-life relationship with Jesus is a fascinating idea. Third, Timothy's prediction of greater acceptance of reincarnation among Christians is a prophecy that is being realized today.

Brother Timothy was certainly not alone in his belief that Jesus had lived an earlier life than the historical one we all know. Commentary by early Christian scholars, evidence that emerges from the philosophy of the first Christian sects, and a few passages from the Bible support this belief.

In John 8:58 Jesus himself says 'Before Abraham was, I am'. Evidence that the Jews expected the reincarnation of their prophets is to be found throughout the Bible. In the closing lines of the Old

Testament we find a prophecy that Elijah, the Hebrew prophet of the ninth century B.C., would return: 'Behold I will send you Elijah the prophet before the coming of the great and dreadful day of the Lord . . .'. And in Matthew 16:13–14 we find: 'When Jesus came into the coasts of Caesarea Phillipi, he asked his disciples, saying, Whom do men say that I the Son of man am? And they said, Some say that thou art John the Baptist; some Elias [Elijah]; and others, Jeremias, or one of the prophets.' Jesus then affirmed his own belief in reincarnation when he told his disciples in Matthew 17:12–13: 'But I say unto you, that Elias is come already, and they knew him not . . . the disciples understood that he spake unto them of John the Baptist.'

When Jesus was confronted with an opportunity to make clear his position on the pre-existence of himself or others, he usually chose to make a more concrete observation. A good example is found in John 9:1–3: 'And as Jesus passed by, he saw a man who was blind from birth. And his disciples asked him, saying, Master, who did sin, this man, or his parents, that he was born blind? Jesus answered, Neither has this man sinned, nor his parents'. It is clear that the disciples had past lives in mind when they questioned the cause of the man's blindness from birth, for if the man were blind from birth he could not have committed a sin in this lifetime. In bypassing this issue, Jesus presented a more pragmatic consideration: healing through belief in the power of God.

The pre-existence of Jesus Christ certainly is not conclusive evidence that reincarnation is a fact of everyone's life. However, we must consider that Jesus constantly reminded his followers that they were his equal in flesh, in spirit, and in deeds: 'Verily, verily, I say unto you, He who believes in me, will do the very deeds I do, and he shall do greater deeds than these'. (John 14:12) Jesus presented himself as an example, not an exception. In his simple, loving ways Christ proved himself to be potential actualized in flesh, and he urged us to recognize that we are too.

In Jesus' time there were three branches of Judaism: the Sadducees, the Pharisees, and the Essenes. The Sadducees did not believe in life after the death of the physical body, but the Pharisees, who were much admired for the strict observance of the Law of Moses, had as one of their chief beliefs the reincarnation of good men (though they felt the bad ones were subjected to punishment instead). The Essenes, a Jewish sect whose communal life was revealed in the Dead Sea Scrolls, are believed by many to have influenced Jesus during those years of his life about which the Gospels are silent. These ascetic Jews may have been in touch with Buddhist monks in the two centuries prior to the birth of Jesus, and they asserted a belief in immortality with strong leanings towards reincarnation. In fact, there is strong evidence of an East–West cross fertilization in the centuries surrounding the birth of Christ – something that was not to happen again in any significant way until our own time.

The Early Christians were naturally influenced by the major branches of Jewish theology; within their own ranks the Gnostics and Neo-Platonists nurtured the concepts of reincarnation. Two men of the early church stand out as proponents of reincarnation. In the second century A.D., Justin Martyr, founder of the first Christian school in Rome, promoted the doctrine of reincarnation in his teachings. Origen, a Greek theologian born about A.D. 185, was 'the most influential of all the theologians of the ancient church, with the possible exception of Augustine,' according to German theologian Adolf Harnack, writing in the eleventh edition of the *Encyclopedia Britannica*. Saint Jerome supported this view by stating that Origen was 'the greatest teacher of the Church after the Apostles'.

Like Brother Timothy, Origen believed and taught that Jesus had existed in human form before he was born of Mary; that Jesus, the Christ personified, represented the culmination of many lives filled with love and self-sacrifice. Origen also taught that the Scriptures should be interpreted figuratively rather than literally, and that souls continue their learning process after letting go of the physical body.

For the four centuries of the Christian Era the doctrine of reincarnation was an integral part of the theology of the Church. Then reactionary forces began to point out to the Church hierarchy the personal responsibility that is the hallmark of this belief. Where would the Church fit into the life of a person who could work out his or her own salvation?

Two dates stand out as significant in erasing the doctrine of pre-existence from Church theology. (*Pre-existence* was the term used at the time; obviously it implies reincarnation.) In A.D. 325 the Council of Nicea met to adopt the present form of the Bible. Wanting to emphasize the necessity of redemption by faith and grace through the acceptance of Christ as Saviour, the Council rejected almost all passages of gospel that made any reference to reincarnation or pre-existence. Then in A.D. 553 the Fifth Ecumenical Council declared the doctrine, as expounded by Origen and his followers, to be anathema (cursed). Though there was a brief flurry of interest during the Renaissance, notably by Erasmus and Giordano Bruno, the Fifth Ecumenical Council put an end to the belief in reincarnation among Christians until quite recently.

While reincarnation was being suppressed in the Western world, it continued to flourish among the millions of adherents of Eastern religions. We can see in the earliest of Hindu classical scriptures, the *Vedas*, written between 1500 and 1200 B.C.: 'The immortal self will be reborn in a new body due to its meritorious deeds'.

The *Upanishads (Approaches)* are a collection of Hindu texts in the forms of parables, maxims, and dialogues which came into existence about 600 B.C. and are concerned with the connections between the human and divine world. In a dialogue between a king and a sage, the wise one says 'Through his past works he shall return once more to birth, entering whatever form his heart is set on.'

Six hundred years later, at about the time of Christ, the *Bhagavad-Gita (Celestial Song)* was written. Together with the *Upanishads* it constitutes the most revered of Hindu scriptures. Part of an epic poem, the *Bhagavad-Gita* is a dialogue between Arjuna and Krishna, chariot companions, as they move into battle. Gradually revealing himself as the Supreme Lord, Krishna tells the nervous young warrior that life and death are of little worth when compared with eternal values:

Wise men do not grieve for the dead or for the living. Never was there a time when I was not, nor thou, nor these lords of men, nor will there ever be a time hereafter when we shall cease to be. As the soul passes in this body through childhood, youth and age, even so is its taking on of another body. The sage is not perplexed by this.

Of the non-existent there is no coming to be; of the existent there is no ceasing to be.

Even if thou thinkest that the self is perpetually born and perpetually dies, even then, O Mighty-armed, thou shouldst not grieve. For to the one that is born death is certain, and certain is birth for the one that has died.

Buddhism envisions the cyclical nature of human lifetimes as a wheel, and the Buddha proposed certain paths to Enlightenment as a means of being forever released from the repetition of these lives. His concept of reincarnation was that of a flame that continues to burn though the material being consumed is forever new. In twenty-five centuries Buddhism has expanded into over thirty Asian countries and more than twenty-two languages. Throughout all of these manifestations of Buddhism – including a recent and significant interest in Zen Buddhism in the United States – Buddhists generally have upheld Enlightenment as the highest state of perfection, and one requiring many lifetimes to achieve.

Outside Asia, some sort of belief in reincarnation appeared among the Druids, and ancient Irish heroes were thought to be reborn. Herodotus, Plato, and Plutarch all referred to the existence of reincarnation in Egyptian belief. In Persia (now Iran) the Zoroastrians professed a belief in animal evolution through rebirth, and later on in human rebirth. In Judaism, the Qabalists have maintained their belief in reincarnation throughout recorded history. In Islam, the Sufis have kept the belief alive since before the time of Mohammed. Today, in all of Asia, throughout the Middle East, and in growing numbers elsewhere there are believers in reincarnation.

All versions of reincarnation presuppose the existence of a non-physical component in human beings; this has generally been referred to as the Soul. Now, however, the disciplines of astronomy, theology, metaphysics, medicine, psychology, physics, and others are converging towards the realization that human beings are *multi-dimensional* – finely tuned organisms that can be understood as constellations of energy fields operating on various frequencies (which we here denote as Body, Mind, Soul, and Spirit).

Dr Leonard Ravitz and Dr Harold Saxon Burr of Yale University School of Medicine believed so strongly that a man or a woman is more than a physical body that they devoted a good part of their lives to the study of human energy fields. They concluded that 'it is the L-field (life field) that supervises the renewal of the cellular structure of the human body every few years. It is the L-field, not the DNA molecule, which molds the new material into the same design as the old.' This, Dr Ravitz feels, helps to explain memory and how we can recall events that occurred many years earlier, even though the molecules have since been replaced several dozen times. Ravitz also reported that at death the L-field withdraws.

Many people prefer to write off the non-physical aspect of human beings as wishful thinking or the romantic remnant of primitive, superstition-filled cultures. These critics are likely to point to the brain as the source of people's creativity and the reason for *Homo sapiens'* dominion over the creatures of the earth. Scientists have tried for years to explore and map the human brain in order to determine how it differs from that of the so-called lower animals. Beginning with comparative studies of size and weight, they moved on to look at brain weight in proportion to total body weight and thence to various studies of the cortex; but, despite persistent efforts, they have been unable to find that totally unique component which would account for the great difference in self-awareness and the ability to conceptualize. If man's superiority was the result of greater brain weight in proportion to total body weight, the small South American monkey would be two hundred times more intelligent than man!

Even electrochemical studies reveal very little difference between the brains of humans and other animals. The human brain is just not different enough to account for the creation of cities, satellites, or symphonies. No matter how it is dissected and measured, there is an elusive element that defies the researcher. That something is Mind, the link between Soul and Body.

From the beginning, whenever humans have contemplated the stars, smiled at their own images in still water, celebrated a good harvest, or rejoiced at the birth of a child, they have used their Minds. It is Mind that makes human beings the only animals aware of themselves, the only animals to have expectations and disappointments, the only animals to spend more time defending the ego than the physical body. It is Mind that provides us with leaps of insight, with knowingness that cannot be produced through reasoning. It is Mind that records feelings – the joys and sorrows, the traumas and triumphs of each lifetime. And when the physical body dies and turns to dust, the Mind carries on its memories as part of the total Self, born anew in a different time, different place.

If we look upon the human being as an energy constellation made up of Body, Mind, Soul, and Spirit, many old controversies can finally be laid to rest. The wars between Science and Religion lose all their fervour when we acknowledge that quantum physics has demonstrated that there is more to the world than what we can see and touch. We now know that the physical body, once considered a solid form, is actually made up of billions of whirling atoms expressing themselves at particular frequencies. We also know that matter can neither be created nor destroyed, only transformed into energy and back once more into matter, again depending upon its rate of vibration. The whole universe is in fact an entity that is constantly pulsating. In this context it matters little whether a Holy Man has a *vision* or a *psychic experience*. Whether we call a certain kind of light a *halo* or an *aura* no longer concerns us when we recognize the energy source from which it emanates.

William A. Tiller, chairman of the Department of Materials Science at Stanford Research Institute, wrote in *Science of Mind* magazine (January 1974): 'I operate on the assumption that man functions on deeper levels of the universe than just the physical level and that this substantial being functions on non-space, non-time levels of the universe. I feel that, on this level, all mankind is part of one vast organism. We only appear to be separate, distinct from each other because of our instruments of perception at the physical level. With our five physical senses, we sense everything by contrast, by difference, so only the differences between us are registered as signal patterns in our brains. The oneness of our being can only be sensed at a deeper level.'

This oneness of our being is the component of humans that we refer to here as Spirit. Spirit is sometimes called God, or Allah, or Brahman, or Prana, or Divine Mind, or Universal Principle – that which is the essence of the universe and is expressed without individuation in everything that exists.

Soul is the particularized form of Spirit, the intangible energy field of each human being that allows Spirit to be manifested on the earth plane. The Soul can also be thought of as the Greater Self; it is our connection with the universe. Few would quarrel with the definition of Soul as the intangible part of man that survives beyond the grave, for this is what nearly every religion teaches. Some would take issue with the Soul's having consciousness in a non-physical world, and there are many, of course, who would dispute the fact that the Soul manifests itself in a wide variety of bodies and physical lifetimes. At worst, a rejection of organized religion can lead a person to reject all that the religion espouses, including the key concept of the Soul.

Experiencing the reality of a past-life regression is an important step in restoring faith in the existence of the Soul, demonstrating that there is some energy system that can exist apart from the physical body. Thus past-life therapy acts directly to alleviate feelings of helplessness, alienation, or loneliness in a vast universe and restores the sense of meaning and connectedness to the world around us.

Helping clients to realize that the universe is Spirit, manifesting in a way our senses can perceive, is an important first step in the therapeutic process. It has been my experience that the client who knows himself to be a multi-dimensional being operating on many levels of reality – to *be* a Soul rather than *have* a Soul – makes the fastest progress through therapy. In the past we have put the cart before the horse when we identified ourselves solely with our thoughts, emotions, sensory input, and ego. The Greater Self (Soul) has been enslaved by the frightened and insecure self (ego) which will go to any length to protect itself against perceived threat.

People who understand that they are multi-dimensional are willing to look at what they are NOT as well as what they are. They are willing to recognize the myths they have been telling themselves through the years. They are willing to go back in time and space to discover the origins of their fears, frustrations, and phobias. They are willing to unleash that dynamic energy of the Self and move forward with a sense of control, choice, and confidence never before felt.

The re-experiencing of past lives releases repressed emotions and frees people to become who and what they really are. They realize that there is no powerful distant Deity smiling down on some and frowning on others. There is no judgement from lofty places after death. Our own personal responsibility is judge and jury every moment of life with or without the body; we choose freely, and the actions we take have their own specific natural consequences. The type of life we choose next is the manifestation of our own 'just desserts'.

When we get in touch with the non-physical Self that always experiences life with objectivity, it helps us to realize that we are the composers, the orchestrators, of our lives. We are also the instruments on which we play. At first we make discordant sounds, but with the practice of many lifetimes we learn to play the music of the spheres. Getting in touch with the non-physical dimensions of the Self helps people to reduce their identification with the physical body, material possessions, and questions of status. They understand that the capacities of the body and the material goods of the earth life are tools to be used for growth and evolution of the spirit. Both good and bad experiences fall into proper perspective and these people are able to stop reacting and take positive action.

It is a common misconception that reincarnation is a straight-line progression; we human beings have a tendency to impose linear constructs on everything we think about. It is necessary to recognize that space and time considerations are arbitrary concepts that we have imposed upon ourselves in order to make our sensory perceptions understandable. Yet all of us are familiar with the ideas of infinity and eternity.

To fully understand our relationship with the Universe we must lay aside considerations of space and time and acknowledge that, in a sense we can only begin to comprehend, everything is happening simultaneously. Thus, every action we take or thought we entertain affects not only this lifetime but all the others we have ever had or ever will have.

As multi-dimensional beings we operate not only on the physical plane but also on higher spiritual planes, and are ultimately in concert with all other creatures of this earth and beyond. Our physical bodies are like the tip of an inverted pyramid, with the Mind, Soul, and Spirit representing ever-widening manifestation of ourselves. Each level has its function, its realm of awareness, and its particular frequency. We become aware of these other aspects of ourselves through many channels, including visions, dreams, voices, thought forms, insights, and intuitions.

For the beginning client who is highly sceptical of any existence beyond the physical, the experience of past-life regression is particularly effective – there is nothing like direct experience to make theory meaningful and real. The sceptic has an experience so profound that it is useless to deny its implications. When the person recognizes for the first time that he or she is a vastly complex being with a meaningful place in the universe, the first step towards wholeness has taken place.

There is a truth that is of great comfort to the sceptic and believer alike: the laws of the universe are in operation whether we believe them or not. However, it is only through an understanding of these laws that we can become the magnificent individuals we are intended to be.

4

A PROCESS EVOLVES

> *New occasions teach new duties; time*
> *makes ancient good uncouth;*
> *They must upward still, and onward,*
> *who would keep abreast of Truth.*
> JAMES RUSSELL LOWELL,
> *THE PRESENT CRISIS*

'If you hypnotize me, will I remember anything afterwards? How does it work? How will it feel?' Marie's whispered questions tumbled urgently over one another, though she could plainly see that I was engrossed in studying for exams and not much interested in talking. Already I had more than enough willing subjects in my growing hypnosis underground, but word gets around quickly on a college campus and Marie was not to be discouraged. Eventually her persistence won my full attention and I noticed that her questions reflected both curiosity and fear, so I agreed to make a date for a session.

Actually I was quite pleased that Marie wanted to be a guinea pig, since she was potentially a good subject. She concentrated well on her studies, was intelligent and trusting, and respected me and my investigations. There was already a strong bond of trust between us.

That Marie felt constrained to discuss hypnosis in whispers tells a lot about the state of the art in Rhode island in the early 1960s. There was very little understanding of the process. The topic was not even respectable cocktail party conversation; most people viewed hypnosis with grave scepticism and some thought it an extremely dangerous form of mind control.

That this attitude persists today among many people, despite the common use of hypnosis in medical and therapeutic settings, both puzzles and amuses me. In our everyday lives we are literally bombarded with hypnotic techniques from morning till night, most of them subliminal in effect. Madison Avenue has perfected a repertoire of coercive tactics that depend heavily on the hypnotic susceptibility of the consumer. We have become so used to these intrusions that we rarely notice them consciously, yet their effects can be lasting and often dangerous.

Any number of ordinary situations may inadvertently induce a light trance state. A rainy drive on a long, straight highway with the windshield wipers moving rhythmically can cause time to lose its meaning and the mind to wander far from the act of driving. Many office workers experience similar sensations in the middle of the afternoon as typewriters click and air conditioners hum. Even colours can produce hypnotic effects. In an English stained-glass factory, employees must be relieved from working with blue glass every few hours because the colour causes changes in their brain waves that result in lethargy. It is no myth that blue is a calming colour!

Many activities that we consider beneficial depend for their success upon our entering a light trance state as we participate in them. Hypnosis is the basis of much, if not all, self-healing. Meditation and prayer are both light states of self-hypnosis, and religious ritual creates a trance state that is comforting in itself and also helps to focus its participants on the tenets of their faith. Most encounter groups and other personal growth organizations utilize a form of hypnosis in their processes. Athletes are achieving new records through the use of self-hypnosis. The hallmark of a good symphony, drama, ballet, or film is that it induces a light trance state which allows people to relax and focus so completely that they are 'carried out of themselves' by the performance.

There is nothing mysterious about hypnosis any more. It is merely a deep state of relaxation wherein the quieting of body and conscious mind allows the person to focus with great clarity on one thing of particular interest. The brain shifts into an alpha state and the right side becomes dominant. The process can be guided by another person or it can be self-induced.

At the time that Marie came to me for her promised session, I had already guided numerous friends through hypnotic regressions to earlier stages of their present lives, but had never tried to lead anyone further back, through the womb experience and beyond to a former life. With Marie the past-life regression was achieved for the first time, and under the dramatic circumstances of a raging thunderstorm!

As we settled down for that first session together the evening was warm and humid and lightning flashed occasionally in the distance. Marie confided that she had butterflies and I made her laugh by telling her just to hurry and relax. She wondered again if she would remember what was about to transpire, and I reassured her that very few people have total amnesia about a session – that in fact most people are totally aware of what is being said and, the first time, they are usually doubting it all the way. I asked her if there was anything special that she wanted to accomplish in this session.

'I've always wanted to know where I lost the ring my grand-mother gave me when I was little', Marie said. We agreed to try to locate the ring and, without much resistance, Marie let herself drift into a hypnotic trance as she focused on the rhythmical sound of my voice.

Not long into the session I grew concerned about the approaching storm. The lightning became brighter and the thunder rolled loudly. I incorporated the sound of the thunder into the suggestions I was making to Marie, telling her that each roll of thunder would deepen her relaxation; this was a technique I was to use many times in the future.

We travelled back through the years of Marie's life to the age of two, when her grandmother had just given her a ruby ring as a gift. I asked Marie where she put it. 'On my finger, where else?', she replied, smiling impishly, eyes still closed. We moved ahead in time several weeks to find that the ring was no longer on Marie's finger, but her brain had recorded all the pertinent information.

'Where have you put it?', I asked again.

'I put it in a safe place where no one would find it.'

'Where?', I persisted.

'Oh, I put it in the bedpost. The top comes off so I can hide small things in there'. Marie showed no recognition of what she had just said, though I was sure she would remember it later. What happened to the bed, I wondered, as the thunder grew still louder. I had to close the windows when the wind suddenly drove sheets of rain into the room. Marie was oblivious to the storm but I was beginning to feel like a character in a gothic tale.

'Now let's go further back in time', I instructed her. 'You are getting younger and younger.' Soon Marie was telling me in great detail about her birth experience.

At that point, I decided to try something I had never done before, to guide Marie back to a past life. While my reading had prepared me technically for this step, it was now my turn to have butterflies. The cassette tape needed to be flipped to Side Two. All was ready.

'Now we are going back even further, Marie. We are going back to a scene even earlier, a scene involving you in another time and place, before you were Marie.'

I am sure she could barely hear me, the thunder was so loud. Marie's face remained expressionless for a few moments as she searched the memory banks of her mind. Then she spoke.

'There are lots of people all around me, and there is a lot of noise. They are all shouting and yelling. Some are singing.'

'And where are you?' I asked.

I'm standing with my mother in the midst of all the noise. We're at the station waiting for the train', a younger-sounding voice replied. I asked her name.

'Mama calls me her strawberry girl and Daddy calls me Redtop. But those aren't my real names.' Marie had some trouble recalling her given name, but finally she said, 'It's Lydia, but I hate that and so does Daddy.'

Under further questioning Lydia told me that 'today', 16 February, was her twelfth birthday. She lived with her parents in

Painesville, but she and her mother had been visiting a sick aunt in Cleveland. This morning they had come to see the arrival of an important person; who it was Lydia did not know.

'What is happening now?' I prompted.

'Mothers are telling their children to stay off the tracks. One fresh boy just tripped another boy and they both fell on the tracks.' I asked Lydia to go ahead in time and describe the visitor.

'He is dressed in black and looks very big on such a little train. He didn't get off the train. That's funny', commented young Lydia. She went on to say that people were very happy, singing and dancing, waving flags. Some were on the roof of the station and others had climbed poles to get a better look.

'Who is it?' I asked her.

'I . . . don't know.' She seemed confused.

'What did your mother call him?'

'She didn't say, but she did say that he should carry his razor with him when he travels.'

More important to Lydia, however, was that she felt hungry. She and her mother had not taken time for breakfast before coming to the station and Lydia's patience was running out. This was especially interesting to me because Marie had come to the session wondering if the heavy dinner she had just eaten would interfere with the hypnosis. Marie was certainly not hungry, but Lydia was starving.

Just as I asked Lydia what else her mother was saying a tremendous clap of thunder shook the building. Hail beat against the windows and the power went out. Suddenly the only sources of light were a lone candle in an adjoining room and the frequent flashes of lightning. My tape recorder switched automatically to battery power, but that spot on the tape is marked only by *my* gasp; Marie was oblivious to it all.

'She says everyone is singing out of tune', she responded to my all-but-forgotten-question.

I decided to take Lydia ahead in that lifetime to the scene of her death. She died at the age of sixty-four from pneumonia and she described the death experience in great detail, using phraseology that I was to hear over and over in the upcoming years. We then ended the session and Marie was returned to present time.

If ever there was an instant convert to reincarnation, it was Marie. Before the session she had never given the idea the slightest thought, but now she had confronted an experience that she could not ignore. Marie was an art major with no real interest in history; she had never heard of Painesville and at first thought she had made up that name because she was having hunger pangs! She had never been to Ohio and had no relatives there. Nothing explained Marie's experience to her satisfaction except one thing: that it was reincarnation made manifest.

Reviewing what had transpired, Marie told me that she had wanted to tell Lydia that the man on the train was Abraham Lincoln, but she could not do it. She felt a very distinct other self speaking through her and she could not intercede. I was to find later that the division of consciousness is a frequent and always fascinating aspect of past-life regression.

Days of excited discussion and research followed this, my past-life regression. A number of interesting facts came to light:

1. On 16 February 1861 Lincoln, riding on a four-car train, stopped at Cleveland amid throngs of cheering wellwishers. The train's destination was Washington D.C., where he was to be inaugurated President of the United States.

2. The train pulled out of the Cleveland station at 9 a.m.

3. Painesville is, indeed, a small town near Cleveland.

4. The comment by Lydia's mother makes perfect sense, since the beard that was to become Lincoln's trademark for the rest of his life was new in February of 1861.

Marie's regression was a signal event for both of us, and I began to guide other people in past-life explorations. At the time I viewed these regressions simply as fascinating glimpses into history, affording both personal and general insights into the broad spectrum of human experience. The recognition of their therapeutic potential was to come a number of years later when I was already involved in counselling.

From the beginning I used hypnotic regressions to help clients uncover the childhood traumas that were hidden in their subconscious memories. It is an easy, pleasant, and efficient way to get at the material which, though hidden, still controls the behaviour of the troubled adult.

The theory that our most traumatic life experiences are repressed from conscious awareness is one that goes back to Freud and Jung. What the ego-self is afraid to recognize consciously is pushed deep into the subconscious. The conscious mind acts as a censor of reality, carefully monitoring what is acceptable and what is not. What is rejected as unacceptable is relegated to the subconscious, which accepts everything without any censorship whatsoever. The material is then out of sight, but not out of mind.

If people attempt to repress large amounts of unpleasant or threatening material, they can become battlegrounds where most of their energy is expended just to hide from themselves. This causes them emotional, and often physical, pain. It is the job of the therapist or counsellor to create a safe environment and provide a technique that clients can use to confront this repressed material and release the negative energy it represents.

I had conducted several hundred regressions before coming to the realization that the traumatic events of childhood are often reminders of older traumas that occurred in past lives. The turning point in my understanding came with a young couple who were experiencing disharmony in their marriage; they had tried traditional marital counselling to no avail, yet they were determined to succeed because they really cared for one another.

Seeing them one at a time, I explored each client's childhood, but we found nothing to account for their present tensions. It occurred to me then that we must push still further back in time to find the basis for their distress. In separate regressions both husband and wife recalled a lifetime in Atlantis in which the man was a scientist of great renown and the woman was his rival. Without knowing what the other had revealed, each reported amazingly similar details of that Atlantean lifetime. Apparently the spirit of fierce competition had not resolved itself over the years, although each person recalled other lifetimes that they had spent together. Exploring the Atlantean lifetime with great care began the process of releasing the negative energy that stood in the way of that couple's present happiness.

Although the client often feels a measure of relief with traditional regression therapy, the complete release from the past is unlikely without returning to earlier events: those that occurred before this lifetime; those that shaped the basic personality before the genetic coding of the new parents and the influences of the new environment.

This is where traditional regression therapy must be seen as a two-dimensional approach, with genes and environment vying for dominance in the shaping of the personality. Past-life regression adds another dimension. Many people have felt the paucity of a theory that tries to account for all the infinite variations of humankind by heredity and environment alone, when we recognize intuitively that there is a uniqueness about each person that goes beyond either. The three-dimensional approach elicits a wealth of information from the client and allows a release of the primary suppression. The release makes way for a revaluation of the ego-self and a realization of other aspects of the multi-dimensional Self.

The therapeutic process that I now call *perception psychology* was born when I realized that its central concept must be the multi-dimensional nature of each human being. The ego-self is only the most obvious manifestation of a multi-dimensional being of much greater complexity. Each person is a finely-tuned energy constellation operating on frequencies of Body, Mind, Soul, and Spirit. Only when all frequencies are in harmony can any of us achieve the freedom and creativity that is our greatest potential.

I was already using both present-life and past-life regression as counselling tools when I discovered the third component of perception psychology: the existence of an objective awareness residing within each of us that is commonly called the Greater Self. (You could also think of it as the Soul – or even the Superconscious). This Greater Self is able to view events of the past, present, and future without regard for time. It is able to view health problems from a spiritual level, to see relationships clearly, and to communicate wisdom that goes far beyond that of the conscious mind.

Many clients have resolved their own dilemmas by allowing this uncensored part of themselves to speak or write (automatic writing) through them while they are in regression. It is not necessary to be in regression to consult this source of knowledge within us. Indeed, many people do so through meditation or self-hypnosis, though they may call it intuition or the inner voice, and all of us do it naturally through waking and sleeping dreams.

In perception therapy the client who has a present sense of helplessness or fear is guided through past events and encouraged to confront situations that were painful, confusing, or threatening. In an atmosphere of safety and trust this person can completely release any repressed hostility which had been directed towards self or others. Myths about life can be recognized and transformed into more accurate perceptions, thus bringing the client closer and closer to personal control and confidence.

Clients are encouraged to view events and people objectively, disassociating them from past experiences and seeing them in a more spiritual light. Options and life directions are analyzed as a natural part of the new awareness. Encouraged to take risks that have formerly triggered the traumatized responses of the past, the client slowly realizes that the past need no longer influence the present. With that awareness, control can be assumed.

The goals of perception therapy are to be free of ego domination, to be free of the past, to live in harmony with all dimensions of the Self, and to be in control of your own personal creation. As one client said, 'It's as if you have always been on automatic pilot and suddenly you find you can take over the controls'.

The process that has evolved for achieving these goals of perception psychology generally falls into eight steps.

Step 1 Setting the Stage

After a preliminary discussion in which we establish the client's reason for seeking help, there is an explanation of the conditions that will be most conducive to success. The person is asked to give up the need to control the situation, to 'edit' the material that arises, or to censor what is revealed. It is important to feel every emotion that comes to the surface and to experience fully all situations that arise. There must be total commitment to this focus, and free expression without any avoidance. All distractions and intruding thoughts must be shelved until the process is completed.

If it becomes evident that the material is being recited without true involvement, or is complicated by distracting thoughts, I instruct the person to 'get inside' the situation, repeating this as often as necessary to make the experience real.

Step 2 The Entry

The second step involves the selection of a specific method or combination of methods that will act as the framework for the release of repressed emotions. The choices include structured hypnosis, guided imagery, self-analogy, and dream re-creation. For most clients, the structured hypnosis is chosen as the appropriate technique.

As part of the technique chosen, key phrases are used to help the client change from sensory to nonsensory reality. Some of these include:

1. Seeing with the inner eye
2. Entering the alpha state
3. Aligning hemispheres of the brain
4. Feeling the head grow larger
5. Feeling the head expand or extend out of the crown area
6. Having a funnel at the top of the head

7. Feeling the whole body to be light and floating
8. Having the brain become a radio that can be tuned to a different station
9. Watching a movie or a play
10. Looking at a computer screen (CRT)

Step 3 The Experience

At some point in this proceeding, regression to a childhood experience will occur spontaneously or the client will allow direction to some such event. The client has now entered a deeper level and the scene is explored fully as a personal experience rather than a simple observation.

Step 4

The scene triggers an earlier scene, and regression to earlier and earlier scenes continues until we reach what seems to be a primal scene in this lifetime.

Step 5

If the birth scene has not been the primal scene, the client is then led back to birth and to the foetal period.

Step 6

A shift occurs at this point into superconscious awareness as the client is regressed to a past-life experience wherein lies the root of the presenting trauma. This is explored as fully as possible, always encouraging the client to experience the emotions that accompanied the incident.

Step 7 The Return

The client is brought back to present time through rhythmic counting interspersed with reassuring suggestions that awareness will be greater than before. I suggest that present barriers can now be seen in the light of past experiences just revealed.

Before regaining full awareness in the present, some clients are receptive to allowing their Greater Selves to speak through them; this can give added insights and perceptions about the material just experienced and often reveals details overlooked.

Step 8   Conclusion

Discussion and analysis follows the regression and brings the session to a close. However, the client is made aware that dreams and flashes of insight may occur for several days or weeks afterwards. These should be recorded and brought to the next counselling session.

This process allows the client to work through the repression and bring to light that which had hidden so long in the shadows. Fears, self-alienation, incompleteness, and helplessness dissipate and are replaced with feelings of wholeness, competency, and completeness.

People become aware of inner strength as the result of seeing themselves as eternal beings who have many lifetimes to work through growth experiences and develop unconditional love for self that is not dependent on the attention, approval, or rewards of others. This is a liberating experience that creates the conditions for full maturity. Other people are seen as complementary to the total acceptance of self; they are no longer seen either as sources of authority or as possessions.

Genuine caring, sensitivity, and interest are essential attributes of the counsellor, but even more important is to be fully present. This presence involves more then perceptive and intelligent listening; it requires the intuitive Self to be fully operational. Since the client is being encouraged to release, the counsellor must also release from consciousness all personal problems and any concerns with time and schedules. If clients view the counselling situation as a harbour of unconditional safety and acceptance, they will contact that portion of themselves which is most important for them to contact.

The counsellor must be a guide, a mirror, a teacher, a listener, and a believer in the potential of full humanhood. In addition, counsellors must be highly intuitive and in touch with all the dimensions of their own beings.

This counselling process is designed to open the door to objective self-discovery and to help the client utilize daily the tools of therapy. On their own, clients can learn to turn inward for the creative strength to build rewarding lives.

5

THE FIVE LEVELS
OF REGRESSION

Dust to the dust! but the pure spirit shall flow
Back to the burning fountain whence it came,
A portion of the Eternal.
He hath awakened from the dream of life.

PERCY BYSSHE SHELLEY, *ADONAIS*

'How deep was I?' seems to be a question of interest to almost all people who undergo regression. Those who have just explored a past life for the first time are quite suspicious of their responses if they remember clearly all that has transpired, and especially if they were consciously evaluating their answers as the regression proceeded. Those who have forgotten all or most of what occurred are even more curious about their degree of involvement when they hear tape-recorded conversations in which they were full participants. It helps most clients to integrate the new experience if they have a way of comparing it to those of other people who have done the same thing.

In order to provide a tool for my clients, and to help myself evaluate what is happening during a regression, I have defined five levels of regression. These distinctions are based on the degree of client involvement and the client's subjective assessment of the reality of the experience.

Level 1 Regression
The most superficial level, this experience is very much like looking at an out-of-focus photograph. Frequently the image is unclear, and

some clients simply have feelings, hunches, or intuitive ideas related to the scene without actually 'seeing' anything specific. Some people describe this level as a peripheral vision; others feel that they are looking through gauze. The scene may shift suddenly, or unexpected elements may suddenly present themselves. Sometimes there appears to be a collage of seemingly unrelated scenes or details.

At this level the client still remains 80 per cent focused on the counselling situation and has shifted only 20 per cent into the past. Distractions are common at this level. A loud sound, slight bodily discomfort, or an intruding thought can break the focus easily and return full attention to the present. If several people are part of the scene from the past, clients at Level 1 have difficulty identifying themselves among the figures they see.

Typical responses taken directly from Level 1 regressions include the following:

1. I'm having trouble telling who I am.
2. I don't know.
3. I can't tell exactly.
4. I think so . . . I feel as though . . . I suppose.
5. It's just not very clear.

A Level 1 regression leads to a Level 2 for most people. Some, however, never let themselves feel safe enough to move into any clear awareness of past trauma. Remaining at Level 1 is a method of avoidance. It is the unconscious safety valve open wide.

Level 2 Regression

Most people, about 75 per cent, are able to move to this level, in which cloudy images are replaced by clear, distinct general images and impressions. Some specific details are also noted. There is no clear identification with a body, however, the usual feeling being that of hovering over the scene with a nonphysical form. Clients may 'try on for size' some visible bodies to see which one feels right. Sometimes there is then a successful identification, other times not.

At this level the focus on the present still accounts for about 60 per cent of attention, with 40 per cent on the past.

Some actual responses from Level 2 include:

1. I'm looking down on the scene.
2. I feel like I'm making this up.
3. The red is so bright.
4. He seems to be just standing there. Why doesn't he do something?
5. She seems to be very sad.

Level 3 Regression

This level is experienced very much like a movie, though there may be some initial detachment from the action. The identification, once made, is quite complete and the other senses are activated. The person may smell the flowers in the garden, hear the crashing waves, feel the sharp sword, or taste the medicine.

At Level 3, which is experienced by about 50 per cent of all susceptible subjects, the person is able to go forward or backward in time, describing scenes from birth to death in the past lifetime. Awareness of the present counselling situation is diminishing more and more, with 40 per cent of attention on the present and 60 per cent on the past.

Sometimes people are surprised by the clarity of their impressions at this level, and they may comment favourably or critically about what they are experiencing:

1. The children are all different sizes in the class. That's funny.
2. There's a fire going in the stove at the side of the room. How nice.
3. There's a man shouting at me. He looks mean.

Other expressions that indicate their degree of involvement are:

1. The rain is pounding on the roof.
2. I feel very dizzy.

3. My foot is caught between the rocks.
4. He could not hear me yelling at him.

Level 4 Regression

About 30 per cent of those undergoing regression achieve Level 4. This client is very much involved in the regression at this level, with much less observation and more participation. All the senses are activated and little analysis or editing is done. The person is able to present numerous details and explain relationships with little difficulty. 'I don't know' is seldom heard at this level. No longer experiencing the double exposure effect of Levels 1 to 3, the person focuses on the past with only an occasional flash of awareness of the counselling situation. Names, places, and dates are given with little hesitation. Only 20 per cent of the client's attention remains in the present.

Level 5 Regression

Here the client is totally involved in the scene from the past and the reality of it is as complete as anything experienced by the conscious mind in this frame. For the 10 per cent of clients who achieve Level 5, all conscious awareness of the present is blotted out by the stronger image from the past. The desire to become the past self is so strong that involvement is 100 per cent.

At this level dialect, accent, mannerisms, and peculiar expressions are evident; a foreign language may be spoken. The emotions of the past self are fully activated and all thoughts are with the mind of the past self. I have been asked by clients at this level 'Who are you?' and 'Why are you here?' (The response 'I am a friend' usually satisfies them, as they are more interested in the scene in which they find themselves and really don't care who I am as long as I am not a threat).

The sense of time becomes distorted at Level 5. After an hour at this level the client may feel that nothing happened at all or that the regression was aborted after only a few minutes. Sometimes, as with Jean in Chapter 1, the client will apologise for falling asleep and wasting my time. Emotions of impatience, anger, and even rage are often released at Level 5. The most potentially provable material also arises from the Level 5 regression.

One of the most distinguishing characteristics of this level is partial or total amnesia of everything experienced in the regression. The repressed material has been relived and released without the observation of the conscious mind. After such a session, people are sometimes amazed to hear their tape-recorded voice giving details of a life that had not been known consciously.

Some representative comments from Level 5 regressions are:

1. My God, I'm trapped!
2. She refuses to listen to me.
3. Oh no, the water is filling my lungs.
4. I've never heard of the United States.
5. I'm dying.

A brief excerpt from a transcript of a Level 5 regression will show the clarity of detail that emerges.

* * * * * *

Are you sitting on the ground?

On the bank of the river.

Are you a man or a woman?

I'll *be* a man.

How old are you?

Thirteen.

What is your birthday?

July 15, 1781.

Do you live in the house you just mentioned a while ago?

Of course.

What is your name?

Judd.

Do you go to school, Judd?

There ain't no school here.

Do you live in a town or a city?

Of course not. Wouldn't do me no good to live in a city since I can't get around anyway.

Why not?

Bad foot.

Has there been an accident of some sort?

No.

Were you born with it?

Reckon so.

*   *   *   *   *   *

It should be noted that very positive results can be obtained even at the lower levels, though most clients would like to experience a Level 5. In fact, many people have the preconceived notion that anything less than a Level 5 is not really hypnosis, because of the myth that hypnosis is unconsciousness or sleep.

No matter what the level of the regression, the client is usually directed to a death experience in the past life, since fear of death (survival concern) often underlies general anxieties and fears that cannot be pinpointed.

(6)

FOOTPRINTS IN THE SANDS OF TIME

Lives of great men all remind us
We can make our lives sublime,
And, departing, leave behind us
Footprints in the sands of time.

HENRY WADSWORTH LONGFELLOW,
A PSALM OF LIFE

What makes a person undergo a past-life regression? Some people come to the Alternative Therapies Council because their friends or relatives have told them of positive changes in their present lives that have resulted from the releasing of repressed materials from former lives. Others may come as a result of my lectures and media appearances, in which I have discussed the concepts and techniques of past-life regression. Still others come to the Alternative Therapies Council for traditional counselling and are at first totally unaware of the opportunity to explore other lifetimes.

Some of the clients have a firm belief in reincarnation, though they may never have experienced a regression. Some have no knowledge of reincarnation but are fascinated by the concept. Many have no interest whatsoever in past lives, and a few are actively hostile to the idea. However, the past emerges with great clarity and relevance for individuals who are unable to accept the idea of reincarnation, demonstrating something stated earlier: the laws of the universe work whether we believe them or not. Nevertheless, it would be unethical on the part of the counsellor and could be harmful to clients to lead them into a regression without their consent. Since genuine growth and development is predicated upon our taking full responsibility for the direction of our lives, there would be no point in imposing the counsellor's views on clients, and the dependency encouraged by such an imposition would only add to their burden.

About half the people who come to the Alternative Therapies Council do so solely to experience a regression. The others wish to deal with specific problems, such as:

1. Feelings of helplessness, unworthiness, purposelessness (withdrawal), and anger (aggression)
2. Stress, free-floating anxieties, nameless dreads
3. Fears, phobias, sense of being trapped
4. Relationships
5. Health problems, pain, lack of energy and motivation
6. Revealing the spiritual Self; learning meditation and self-hypnosis
7. Addictions and compulsions
8. Talents; creative blocks
9. Occupational dissatisfactions
10. Sexual difficulties

For the first-time subject, the adventure of a regression is often filled with excitement and anticipation mixed with anxieties about the new experience. People bring with them many misconceptions about hypnosis, so the first step must be to explain it thoroughly and to eliminate the myths that have grown up around it. I explain that hypnosis is an altered state of consciousness – a deliberate, attentive listening done in an atmosphere of trust and relaxation. The term *hypnosis* is actually misleading, since it comes from the Greek word meaning sleep; hypnosis is no more sleep than apples are oranges. Even those subjects who go to the deepest levels of hypnosis are never asleep, for they are responsive to all statements by the hypnotist. Hypnosis and sleep do share one common element: they are both altered states of consciousness that allow the use of inner senses rather than outer ones.

Responses to hypnosis vary with the individual, but for most people certain sensations are very common. Some of the most often noted sensations are: heaviness, lightness, dividedness, separation, expansion, rising, falling, time distortion, numbness, enhanced alertness, keen focus and perception, electrification, tingling, pulsating, turning, spinning, freedom. Inner senses are stimulated to produce intense light and colours, flashing lights, buzzing or clicking sounds, ringing, and other auditory and visual manifestations. Hypnosis is different for everyone and there is no single phenomenon to describe it.

'You are not going to believe this' may be the most common statement I hear from a client; it is usually followed by the description of some experience beyond the five senses and the hesitant admission that 'I think I may have been in another lifetime'.

Another comment that crops up repeatedly is 'I don't think I'll be a good subject'. This conveys to me the client's feelings of self-deprecation, modesty, expectation reduction, or even avoidance. That is, however, quite different from the statement of challenge embodied in 'I bet you can't hypnotize me!' My unvarying response to such a challenge is 'That is very true, since I have never hypnotized anyone in my life. No one can hypnotize someone else. All hypnosis is self-hypnosis, even when there is guidance by another person.' Willingness and trust are the key ingredients that allow this self-hypnosis to occur. Belligerence or a 'see if you can do it' attitude are not conducive to hypnosis.

Sometimes clients are concerned that they may be harmed by 'tampering' with the past, but unless the encounter is experienced with fear, there is no danger. This is just as true of past-life exploration done under the guidance of a professional as it is of the same work done on one's own through self-hypnosis. Emotional states colour everything we experience, so regressions must be approached with a positive mental attitude. For most people, a first experience with the past is best undertaken with a professional, who then gives post-hypnotic directions for independent work. For those interested in working on their own, a later chapter gives directions and suggestions for doing so.

Reliving past lives in a counselling situation may not feel as unusual as you anticipate, since glimpses of past lives occur both daily and nightly for most of us. While conversing with a friend we may suddenly see some unexpected expression or distortion of features, or the superimposing of one face over the other. In a particular locale we may have a strong sense of familiarity or belonging. Becoming engrossed in a historical film or novel can trigger memories of other times and places. In daydreaming we may suddenly realize that we are seeing a parade of faces and scenes, only to find that they vanish just as we become aware of them. Dreams experienced during sleep contain elements of past lives, often like a collage of past, present, and future. Only very rarely does a dream unfold a full past-life sequence. (Since there is no awareness of time in altered states of consciousness, past, present, and future are all *now*.)

Why don't we remember past lives in the same way as we remember incidents that happened earlier in this lifetime? Apparently there is some agreement that the lessons of this lifetime are to be learned without reference to the past experiences until a certain level of development is attained. It is well-known that infants and young children often refer to things that could only have happened in a former lifetime. Almost without exception the adults around them will go to great lengths to convince the child that the experience could not have occurred; it is not long before the child begins to conceal such memories and soon has learned to suppress the awareness from which they sprang. The interesting thing is that it is apparently just as easy to open yourself again to the greater awareness of an infant as it was to suppress it when the world told you to do so. There is nothing stronger than potential unleashed.

People experience little difficulty in moving back into the physical reality of the counselling situation after a past-life regression. It is a simple shifting of focus back to what is most familiar and secure. In working with thousands of cases, I have never seen a person have more than momentary difficulty adjusting to the present time. The intrusion of another self passes quickly, and is invariably gone a few hours later. Dreams are sometimes more vivid after a regression and they sometimes reveal further information about the past life that has been explored. Even in the waking state the conscious mind may be temporarily flooded with the elaboration of the information that came up during the session. This is always experienced as pleasurable and satisfying to the aroused curiosity.

Nearly everyone expresses an element of disbelief just after a session, typically saying 'I feel that I was making it up'. This feeling may persist through several regressions even though the past-life material is beyond the experience and knowledge of the client in this lifetime. Despite this feeling of unreality, when research into the factual data of regression confirms its accuracy, the client is not surprised. Characteristically, a regression produces mixed feelings: It was real, and yet not real; I was there, and yet I was still here; I was thinking with the mind of that earlier self, yet my present mind insisted on editing what was going on. Much of this confusion arises from the erroneous belief on the part of most clients that they will not be conscious of their surroundings or have knowledge of this life while they experience others. Sometimes they will not, but especially at first they are likely to remain aware of their physical surroundings and the counselling situation.

A skilled hypnotist begins the induction process from the moment the client enters the office by guiding the conversation in such a way as to reduce stress and anxiety while increasing the person's receptivity to dealing with past energies and present emotions. After discussing the reasons for the client's choice of a regression experience, we do some preliminary exercises on visualization and the analysis of analogies. Susceptibility to hypnotic trance is generally evident by this time, though it may be necessary to allay the person's worries about being a poor subject.

Some people come to a counselling session too sleepy or too stimulated for effective work. The stress of the issues at hand is always compounded by taking excessive stimulants such as coffee or relaxants such as alcohol, and there is a concomitant lack of ability to focus. When this happens there is nothing to be done except to reschedule the session.

When the preliminary discussion is completed, the client is asked to embark on a guided journey for which the counsellor will be the navigator. It is essential that both client and counsellor agree to trust one another and to focus on the agreed-upon areas of distress. The client is then directed to relax the physical body, paying attention to each part individually, beginning with the eyelids and progressing down to the toes. Some people are able to proceed rather quickly with this, while others – particularly those who are unfamiliar with relaxation techniques – require guidance at a slower pace.

After the body is relaxed and the arms and legs are limp, attention is directed to the breathing. I state that with each breath the relaxation will become more pronounced and that there will be a feeling of numbness and lightness. The next step is to quiet the conscious mind. The client is asked to imagine pulling the plug of the mind's computer or erasing the blackboard of thought. These are images that can be visualized quite easily by almost everyone. There is the further suggestion that all thoughts that try to intrude during the induction will be erased immediately, as will all sounds that might prove distracting.

The key phrases 'letting go' and 'relaxing deeper and deeper' are repeated many times and there is a continuing focus on breathing. Effort to produce deep hypnosis at this time is unnecessary and sometimes gets in the way. If a client is having a particularly hard time relinquishing control, it usually helps to encourage 'Just as deep a state of relaxation as possible'. After five to fifteen minutes, most clients are ready to move backwards in time. I usually use the image of the clock with hands spinning backwards rapidly. Often the years are counted as the client is 'getting younger and younger'.

At this point the person is asked to stop at any scene that carries the emotions of the problem brought into counselling. Most people are able to find incidents of childhood quite easily that pertain to the issue at hand. Some find so many that the entire session is used to explore these times and events. Often the tie-in to the present problem is not obvious to the client, who is fully involved in the scene, sometimes to the point of tears or laughter. After such an encounter, most clients comment that they did not think they could 'remember' their childhood experiences so well. Many are puzzled by the vividness of the images and the feelings that seemed so real.

Usually people are so eager to get to past-life material that they move rather quickly through the childhood memories. Depending on their primary interest, we may omit the birth and womb experiences to allow more time for other lifetimes. When the client is both relaxed and responsive, we are ready to go back still further into the past. One useful image at this point is that of a dark tunnel through which one seems to be comfortably floating. The suggestion is made that the end of the tunnel opens onto a scene from an earlier life. The client then has the opportunity to focus on that scene before entering and becoming a part of it.

In the following regression, I have just told Arnold to look at the scene at the end of the tunnel. He had come for a regression out of curiosity and was planning to do others later on. I asked some questions to get verifiable facts, but there was no attempt to concentrate on that aspect of it. Arnold wanted to cover as many kinds of things as possible and we planned to discuss his responses later, as you will see.

*   *   *   *   *   *

The scene becomes clearer and clearer. What are you looking at?

It's a woman praying at an altar.

I see. Tell me everything you are aware of.

We're in a large old church, long narrow windows, stone arches, a large round stained glass window in the front.

Do you feel that you are alone?

There are only the two of us in there.

How is the woman dressed?

White gown with green trim, long lace . . . feeling uncomfortable . . .

Tell me how you are dressed.

I'm wearing a red shirt. Been working outside, hands are dirty.

You are a man?

Yes. I'm waiting for her to finish praying. Don't like the church much.

Who is this woman?

She's Ann.

Her name is Ann? You call her Ann?

Yes.

And what does she call you?

She calls me Jay. My name is Jason.

I see. Is Ann related to you?

No.

Is she a friend?

Yes.

And you've come here with her?

No, I came . . . I knew she was inside, so I came in looking. I don't think I'm supposed to be here, but I know a back door. I work on the grounds.

You work on the grounds. You're a gardener?

Yes.

What is your last name, Jason?

Leopold.

You said you didn't care much for the church. Can you tell me why?

The people, they're . . . they speak of love all the time . . . I do not see it in them at all.

Has the Church hurt you in some way?

It seems God is for the rich people.

And yet you work for the Church. Why do you do that?

I work for different . . . whoever calls me, I work for them. I work for the Church only when there is no other work to be found.

I see. And do you get paid in money for your work?

By the Church, yes. I also work for a nobleman and he gives me a place to stay.

How much will you get paid for the work?

Uh . . . two shillings a day.

And you get paid at the end of each day?

Yes. Just as it gets dark another fat monk or priest comes out and pays me.

Can you tell me what the payment looks like?

Two coins. Brown in colour.

What is the name of this place we're in at the moment? What is this area called?

Coventry.

What country is this?

England.

What season of the year are we in at the moment?

Autumn.

Do you know today's date?

It's November. I'm not sure what day.

What year is it?

1747.

Do you know who the ruler of the country might be? Who is on the throne? Who do people talk about?

They talk about King George.

Do they talk about anyone else?

Mostly about [sigh] noble people . . . we talk about the noble people. The nobleman I work for is named Frederick . . .

That's in Coventry?

Yes.

Have you ever been outside of England?

No. Ann would like to take me to France.

Why?

Oh, to get away from here [sigh]. We have a relationship that is . . . people don't like it.

Why is that?

[Sigh] I'm not of proper breeding for her. She is . . . the daughter of the nobleman.

How old are you, Jason?

I'm 27.

How old is Ann?

She is the same.

I see. Have you ever been outside of Coventry?

Mmm, no. When I was young I was in . . . city named York . . . something . . .

What was it?

It was named York.

Do you know why you were there?

I was born there . . . such a long time ago . . . his brother took custody . . . the nobleman. I was raised like the workers that belonged to the nobleman . . . or worked for the nobleman. He did not raise me in his home since I was not of family.

I see.

I met Ann four years ago, working in the garden at the back of his large house.

If you were to go to France with Ann would you go by airplane?

. . . Can't travel by air. Would take a wagon, my old wagon, and then maybe go to the shore. She knows a fisherman and he will take us. I have an old wagon. Have to dress her up a little bit different. There's one road I've never been down before . . . would be the first time I'd ever been down this road . . .

Have you ever heard of anyone travelling by air?

No. I've heard of people who claim they fly in their sleep . . . large bags I've heard of in France . . . fly in the air . . . I don't believe that.

Do you think that man will ever really fly?

Oh, yes. I believe anything to be possible . . . Church doesn't, however . . . that's one of the reasons I do not like to associate with them.

Do you think you and Ann will be together?

Yes. We really want to. I'm always afraid of what the people say . . . and she, what kind of life would she have . . .

Do you do any other kind of work?

Yes, I'd like to learn to work with wood.

With wood?

In my spare time I would cut branches into different figures.

Tell me what you look like.

Dark hair. I've got a scar on my cheek, I think from a fight many years ago. I seldom get to see what I look like. In the nobleman's large house there is glass and then I can see myself . . .

Is it glass intended for seeing yourself?

Yes . . . many of those.

Are you tall, short, or average?

I don't know. You could call me tall, but there are taller people than I am.

How much would you say you weigh?

I don't know. They weigh in stones . . . I don't know what kind of stones they use . . . or how many of them I weigh.

I see. What sort of work do you do for the nobleman?

He has a small creek in the back, and I keep the edges clean and branches . . . there shouldn't be any branches growing into the water [sighing] . . .

What else do you do?

Ah . . . seems I move stones for the nobleman. I'm not sure he knows what he wants . . . move stones back and forth . . . I find this to be very unpleasant. If I would move the stone once, I would leave it, but he wants me to move it there and there and . . . I have to put some stones into a boat and then carry them.

You said this nobleman's name was Samuel?

No, his name is Frederick.

Let's go ahead in time and see whether you are going to be with Ann. It's several years ... you're getting older ...

We are living together now in Holland.

You've moved across the water to Holland?

Yes, but I've been here for a while by myself. She grew very ill in England and sent me alone [sigh]. She said it would be for the best if I went first. Maybe the illness was God's will and that I should go by myself ... led me to be suspicious ... I'm in Holland, not France.

What is it?

Holland, not France. We went by ... fisherman. I and four others went by ourselves. She was supposed to join me.

Ann was supposed to join you?

Yes, in a few months, but it was a few years.

How old were you when she joined you?

Thirty-one.

Are you happy living with Ann?

Oh, yes.

Do you have any children?

Yes.

Can you tell me about them?

There are four of them. One was born prior to when she was married to me.

Is that one your child? Are you the father of that child?

No. In England she was to marry ... and she did marry one ... she was writing to me, but the letters were a long time arriving.

Why is that?

. . . come across on the boat. And she wrote and she stopped writing. It was a very painful thing for me . . . wrote again that she had married someone with noble breeding [sighing] . . . her family caused her to do this.

Then you never expected to see her again?

I . . . did expect to see her . . . inside I felt that way, but nevertheless it hurt.

Then what happened to her husband?

She left him. He did not love her. The noble people do not marry for love.

Has Ann fully recovered? Is she well?

Oh, yes. I prayed for her every day.

Let's go ahead in time some more. Let's go right up to the time of your death, the very moment. Tell me about it.

I'm alone. People know I am to die.

How old are you?

Sixty years old.

What are you dying of?

Just tired. Ann died . . .

When did she die?

Four years ago.

And you know you are dying?

Yes. I wanted to die for a long time. Since Ann died, one of our children died. She was drowned.

Tell me about your death. Tell me about the moment of death. What was this like for you?

[Sigh] Feeling of . . . not quite certain. Somehow never leaving and . . . want to get up and open the door and see the other people . . . Doesn't seem like it's possible not to be able to do that no more. I'm very much afraid.

Let's go to a few moments after your death.

[Sigh] I see cabinet . . . standing over against the wall . . .

The cabinet is standing against the wall?

Yes. That was in the room.

How can you see that if you've just died?

I . . . don't believe I have died . . . but I'm not with the body there lying on the bed.

You can see your body?

This has happened to me before.

What do you mean, this has happened to you before?

I dreamed that I fly and I see my body. I feel I'm dreaming again. Feels like I'm flying a little further, though, from my body than before.

Is your body still alive or is it dead?

I do not care.

You do not care?

No.

What form do you have? What substance are you?

It's difficult to describe. I feel like I have my wings, and yet it feels like my mind and my thinking are in all of my limbs at the same time. I feel like I can see with my feet . . . I feel like I can . . . but yet I can see different things at once. My whole being feels like my head felt formerly. It feels, when I think, everything is thinking.

What was the transition to the death state like? What was it like the moment you crossed into this experience?

It was very light, a light feeling. Was like a change of . . . change of wind . . . the wind changed directions and it . . .

Like the wind changed direction?

Yes, and everything else was the same. Feeling things from a different side.

Were there any voices or anyone calling your name?

Mmm, no. I felt very lonely, but yet I still feel this was only temporary. It was my choice to be by myself. I want to see only one person . . . Ann . . . I wonder if I can see her now . . . I wonder . . .

Can you see her now?

Eyes are in the room. I cannot see her, I feel . . . I feel her waiting off somewhere in the corner of the top of the room. . . through the ceiling . . . perhaps somewhere above the house. Off, off in the corner, away from the bed . . . not in the room, but outside the house . . . I feel she is there.

Let's go ahead in time now. Let the months and the years fly by now . . .

[Sigh]

* * * * * *

With positive suggestions that he would feel relaxed and refreshed, I brought Arnold back to present time. The discussion we had following his regression gives an idea of Arnold's perception of the experience.

* * * * * *

How long did it feel to you, Arnold?

Twenty minutes, not even that. [His voice had changed when he was Jason, but now it was Arnold's voice once more.]

It was about an hour and ten minutes.

[Laughing] Can't be more than fifteen or twenty minutes!

Surprising, isn't it?

Yeah. When I see the room again, it's like I'm . . . I feel like I've really been in the past.

Did you have any connection with reality as you were experiencing the other lifetime?

At the beginning, the truck noise . . . I don't know.

But you were able to get yourself back into that other place?

I don't remember, uh, fading out, being aware of it too much. Hard to describe your voice before, but it was like part of the scenery, just like it was supposed to be there through the whole scope of things . . . something that was following me around all the time.

You had no fear of it or of invasion of privacy?

No. But sometimes I wanted to experience something a little longer and you said move on now . . . like I wanted to stay in that church much longer. I wanted to stay there and take it all in.

Did you feel a need at any time to question who I was or what the voice was?

Just that feeling of acceptance . . . it's hard to describe. Well, at the beginning I was wondering . . . the conscious mind, whatever, I was kind of wondering whether or not what I was saying would be historically verifiable or not. Then I forgot about that and just allowed anything to come in.

Do you remember what name you gave for yourself?

Yeah. Jason . . . no . . . Jas . . . Jason Leopold.

When I asked you about the airplane, how did you feel inside when you were answering that?

Half and half sort of feeling. The first feeling was that it didn't make sense . . . there's a kind of question mark when the word *air* came. And then on the other hand, I guess there must have been my present consciousness.

So first you were thinking with the brain of Jason?

Yeah.

Then you were thinking with the brain of Arnold, is that right?

Yeah, I think that's the way it was. Yeah, the Jason thing was much shorter, just a brief question mark, kind of. I don't remember how long I talked about it, but . . . well, the conscious me was thinking airplane and I was remembering that there were balloons . . . hot air balloons.

But you called them bags.

Yeah. That was the first word I got. I didn't think of the word balloons . . . balloons didn't strike me.

Can you tell me, Arnold, is there anything in your experience in this lifetime that would cause all of this to be formulated as imagination? Have you been to Coventry, England, or travelled in Holland?

I've just been to southern Germany, that's it. Never to Holland or England. Coventry I have heard of. I got a strong feeling about that place in Portland about four years ago . . . I saw a place there that was about a hundred years old and was owned by some nuns, and I had the strange feeling that my family was interested in buying it . . . when I was there it was like I had seen something like it before. I remember that now . . .

And that was like what in the regression?

Well, my conscious . . . Arnold . . . thought well, this kind of looks like the place in Portland.

What looks like the place in Portland?

The house of the nobleman . . . in his house, not the church.

Well, I'm sure you saw more than you described?

Oh, yeah, a lot of neat things. A fence, with a stone wall and a road beyond that. I felt that the estate was not too far from the church, maybe you could even see it. When I was by the cemetery by the church, I remember different consciousness was coming into me and I was questioning it. That happened more frequently the first half. Like the part about the house. I wondered if anyone who lived back then used the word *house*. When I said the glass, looking at myself I was aware of the word *mirror* . . . I could have said the word *mirror* easily, but on the other hand there was a feeling that I didn't know what the word meant.

How about when you talked about weighing in stones?

That bothered me, too. My conscious would get into me and I just suddenly didn't know. My conscious mind thought of pounds and all of a sudden I saw images of stones . . .

So it was the Jason mind that was flashing on stones and it was the Arnold mind that was thinking of pounds?

Yeah, it was hard to differentiate the two sometimes. Sometimes I wish I knew more . . . for my conscious mind I wish I knew more information.

But it makes it more legitimate if you don't. This is interesting. So it wasn't the conscious mind that was feeding back to Jason the idea of stones, it was coming in the opposite direction. Your conscious mind was not saying to Jason, 'Look, you must be talking about stones, not pounds'.

No, no. It was . . .

Seems to be the other way around from what you said?

That's right.

* * * * * *

Arnold's first regression was mostly on Level 4, and he responded easily with a wealth of information and detail. As his follow-up comments indicate, he did engage in some self-editing, though he was enough involved in the past life to reject concepts from his present conscious mind during the regression. An interesting side note was his recognition that a house he had recently seen in Portland resembled the one in which he lived while working for the nobleman in the former life. On seeing the house in Portland he had made up his mind that his family might be interested in buying it, note knowing then that it was the past-life connection that ruled his thoughts. People do, of course, often choose houses or land based on past-life attractions.

Though he disliked his job and was a frustrated lover in the first part of the regression, Arnold had been reluctant to leave that scene when he, as Jason, was asked to move forward to a later time. The death experience he recalled is typical of many, and will be discussed separately in a later chapter.

Arnold's first regression was a successful one in many ways. He returned to a life in which he had a deep and abiding love for his mate, one that left him with a pleasant feeling of nostalgia. Any fear of death was mitigated, if not dissolved, by his recalling this death as a 'shift in wind direction'. Not all regressions bring forth such happy memories, yet all contribute positively to self-knowledge and growth.

THE SOUL'S DIS-EASE

For of the soul the body form doth take:
For soul is form, and doth the body make.

EDMUND SPENSER,
AN HYMNE IN HONOUR OF BEAUTIE

Not too many years ago the word *psychosomatic* became a fashion-able and convenient label for physical complaints that did not fit neatly into the known system of medical diagnosis and treatment; any ailment without some discernible physiological basis could be explained away with the word. Used properly, the term referred to disease originating in the mind (or more precisely, in the brain) and manifesting in the body. However, the shortened expression, 'It's all in your head' was heard with increasing frequency and frustration by many unhappy patients, especially since little help was offered them beyond stern, moralistic admonitions to 'shape up'.

Today's research is demonstrating more and more conclusively that much, if not all, disease actually does begin in the mind (brain). A fleeting thought that generates an emotional response can throw the body into fight-or-flight, the primitive physical reaction to threat; defence mechanisms are activated, hormones and enzymes flow in massive quantities, and the most vulnerable area of the indi-vidual's body takes the brunt of this onslaught.

Ruth, a sixty-year-old woman, had a hearing problem that had been getting worse over the past ten years, and it was very much worse in the year preceding her visit to me. No medical reason could be found after extensive testing. In regression she found herself living in a South American farm community, a member of a very religious family. Her father in that lifetime was a part-time preacher who infused his entire family with the gospel of fire and brimstone. Ruth did her best to shut him out by blocking his voice.

In this lifetime Ruth is a real estate agent, married to a man who is a father image from the past. Her husband constantly preaches to her, trying to make her feel guilty. Understandably irritable from these attacks on the home front, Ruth found her work debilitating. 'I'm tired of hearing my clients' complaints', she said repeatedly in our sessions. Her body was taking Ruth's words literally. This, combined with the negative response pattern from her former life, was taking its toll. After a number of sessions, Ruth realized that she could no longer escape the unacceptable through hearing loss; she had to face people and conditions, and deal with them as effectively as she could. The hearing problem stabilized after the first session and in two years has shown no further deterioration. Occasionally Ruth reports that it has improved somewhat.

A chronic pattern of defensive behaviour such as Ruth displayed has a decidedly negative impact on the individual's health. There are a progression of warning signals ranging from the most subtle, intuitive awareness to physical manifestations of slight discomfort, to pain, to organic or mental breakdown. Ultimately, if these signals are ignored and the cause of the behaviour is not removed, death will result.

Emotions, like thoughts, arise in the brain, and the combination of thoughts and emotions establishes the condition known as *stress*. Stress can be either positive or negative, depending upon our needs, expectations, and prior experiences. Positive stress motivates us, drives us into *action*. Negative stress, on the other hand, drains and debilitates us; it is both a cause and an effect of *reaction*. All stress affects the body, but negative stress certainly weakens the body's resistance. (Consider the positive stress of getting married, the ambivalence of a new job, and the negative stress of a funeral).

Disease, the result of unresolved stress, is an example of the universal principle of cause and effect in operation on many levels of

Self. Dolly was having chronic problems with dizziness and lack of balance, though there seemed to be no physical explanation for her condition. She regressed to a scene in an English village. It was October 1918, and the girl of that lifetime chattered happily to me about the prices charged by village merchants. Suddenly she began to feel dizzy and sick, and nothing I said seemed to relieve what she was feeling or get her beyond the experience. Finally she responded by going to the moment of her death, which had occurred shortly after the onset of these symptoms. Apparently the girl died in the influenza epidemic of 1918, and was buried along with many others in specially dug graves outside the church cemetery. The unexpectedness of her death added to the unconventional burial to produce an emotional trauma that Dolly carried with her still in this life. Fortunately the regression was enough to release her from any further symptoms.

Illness manifests itself only when we have failed to notice or to heed early warning signals. In this physical world we become so dazzled by our senses – so absorbed in what we see, hear, smell, taste, and touch – that we tend to overlook messages from our bodies, which are subtle and often symbolic. These unheeded messages become increasingly obvious the longer they are ignored, until finally they produce symptoms distressing enough to require professional treatment. For example, a man may have a feeling of general uneasiness while eating an acidic food like tomatoes but fail to relate one to the other. Weeks, months, or years later he may begin to notice occasional discomfort in his stomach. A long way down the road, the man may develop an ulcer. At any point along the way, greater awareness of self might have interrupted the process of disease.

Unfortunately traditional medicine has come to depend on drugs and on surgery to heal the body. While some remarkable success has been achieved in this way, there is an insidious side effect of this emphasis that is beginning to be recognized. Both types of treatment encourage passivity in the patient. No personal responsibility for healing is vested with the patient, where it properly belongs; symptoms may be relieved, but this treatment deals with effect and fails to get at cause. As a result, healing is often temporary, and both physical and psychological dependencies may be developed by the patient. In choosing traditional remedies, we often trade off valuable learning experiences for temporary relief, and are soon facing the same challenges when illness strikes again.

When Barbara first came to see me, she was in a great deal of mental and physical anguish. Married to a Vietnam war veteran who himself had severe emotional problems stemming from the war, Barbara was experiencing the conflict between her responsibilities to support and help her husband and her responsibility to herself. It was the sort of situation where none of the options she perceived held any satisfaction for her. In addition, she was suffering from a severe back problem and acute liver disease.

Our preliminary discussion revealed that her husband had threatened to leave several times, but Barbara would not let him go because she felt guilty about not helping him to resolve his problems. Violent from the beginning of the relationship, he once went through a plate glass window during a fight. Because she took one horrified look at the bloody result and then ran for help, Barbara had been berating herself for not staying on the scene and coping with the situation herself.

Since she was ruled by guilt in her marriage, as in other personal relationships, it is not surprising that the liver and back problems were activated. In regression, Barbara recounted a series of lifetimes wherein she had abused the use of alcohol; in this lifetime she had developed such an allergy to alcohol – particularly wine – that her liver was constantly inflamed and enlarged.

Severe back pain was traced to a lifetime in which Barbara had been a strong, physical man. As she looked at a scene where she was a sailor on a ship, she saw a fight start. A man 'with intense hate' about him holds a heavy pipe in his hand, and suddenly he strikes the burly sailor in the back, apparently killing him. Further back, Barbara finds that she was also attacked by a knife in the back during an Egyptian lifetime.

After a number of sessions, Barbara took her first step towards health by leaving her husband (who was, in any case, in and out of hospitals most of the time). She practised the technique of gathering white light from the farthest reaches of the universe and concentrating it on the liver and on the point where she had been struck in the back. As her guilt diminished and she followed the visualization techniques, Barbara improved in almost all the aspects of her life.

True healing is an active process, requiring the combined focus of our physical, mental, emotional, and spiritual energies. The entire Self must be involved if healing is to take place.

The emotions are among the most creative tools at our disposal, and no healing can occur without complete emotional involvement. To be active healers of ourselves, we must be at least as emotionally involved in the cure (eradication of the effect) as we were in creating the condition for the illness (establishing the cause).

No one can heal us, and we can heal only ourselves. Health professionals can help us in the process, but we are ultimately responsible for doing the healing – whether it be an unexpected cold, chronic migraine headaches, or infectious hepatitis. Bringing all our positive energies to bear on a health problem is far more efficacious than any external agent can be; this has been dramatically illustrated time and again in studies where placebos produced the same results as drugs especially developed to cure certain symptoms or diseases. Belief and personal responsibility are the cornerstones of healing.

So much emphasis has been placed on the treatment of disease that little time has been spent on trying to prevent it. If we would wake up to our early warning signals – some of which are evident in dreams, in the analogies we use in everyday speech, and in unobstructive and seemingly general anxieties – we would be able to resolve the negative energy that produces disease. It is one of our most important responsibilities to ourselves and to others.

Growing interest in some medical circles in holistic treatment – that is, treating the whole person rather than the presenting symptom – is heartening evidence that we are beginning to take steps in the direction of recognizing the true origins of disease and the identity of the true healer, the Self.

Traditional medicine has generally ignored the influence of the past, and especially of past lives, on disease and illness, because validating the connection through laboratory controls is next to impossible. Perhaps the best work done so far has been the research of Dr Ian Stevenson into the remembrances of young children. He has found that these children, while completely awake and conscious, are able to recall in great and often verifiable detail the events and circumstances of past lives. (My belief is that there is much in the universe that is not provable because of the inherent limitations of our current research modes, but that in time we will discover the appropriate tools necessary to establish the validity of ideas that are still relegated to conjecture or faith.)

Many present stresses were born in the past, and repression prevents the original circumstances from entering our conscious minds. The incidents were originally painful, and the fear of pain keeps them buried below consciousness, though they continue to dominate our present behaviour. Each day these hidden traumas cause a certain amount of stress, which is compounded by the fear of conscious recognition and repeated pain. Unfortunately we sometimes allow personal fulfilment to be blocked by fear, guilt, and regret, which keeps the door shut on any conscious knowledge or release of old hurts.

Vincent was plagued by deep depressions that impaired his concentration to the point that his business was falling into ruin. He was being treated with anti-depressant drugs, but they had little effect. In regression he returned to a life in England where he was one of the workers who helped to build the *Titanic*. When that 'unsinkable' ship went down, he blamed himself, becoming convinced that it was the poor quality of his work that had made the huge ship vulnerable. After three sessions, Vincent was totally recovered from the depression based on guilt that had carried over from a former life. Looking back, he realized that the depressions had begun when his wife and some friends tried to persuade him to invest in a boat.

Past-life regressions often wedge the door open and allow confrontation with that hidden but strongly influential energy, whether it manifests as a recurring pain that goes back to the eighteenth century, or obesity that had its origin in the fifth century B.C. In fact, obesity is often connected to food deprivation or even starvation in a former life. One person who came to counselling for obesity regressed to a nineteenth-century life where as a four-year-old named Mary Ann, she had crossed the American West in a wagon train. The scene she recalled most vividly was one bitterly cold night just before Christmas. Mary Ann huddled with her younger brothers by the campfire, terrified, while they waited for the men to return from a search for game to eat. At that moment the cold, the fear, and the hunger were nearly overwhelming to the little girl, and she carried the memories all the way to the present.

Anther person who had tried unsuccessfully to lose weight had also suffered from those harsh winters on the Plains. This woman recalled a life as an Indian brave whose responsibility it was to lead his nomadic tribe to settle where the food supply was adequate. It was a heavy burden that became greater each year as the herds of buffalo disappeared.

Also beset by weight problems, Jeanne regressed to life as a serving girl at the court of Louis XVI. She recounted court life in vivid detail, describing the menus, the clothes, and the social occasions at Versailles from the perspective of a servant who dare not look directly at the King. Eventually she married a footman and they 'retired' to a tiny farm that had belonged to her husband's father. Jean-Louis, the husband, died at the age of sixty-three, and Jeanne was left on her own. With no one to help her, she found it impossible to run the farm, and all their friends were too far away. There was nothing to eat, and Jeanne died of starvation not long after her husband. She told me that her body was discovered by a pedlar who came to the house to try to sell something. 'He knocked on the door, and when no one answered, he went in and found my body', she recalled. 'He said "Ah, mon dieu!" and ran away.' Not surprisingly, Jeanne had food deprivation and abandonment firmly connected in her mind, and she always ate when she felt lonely or rejected.

Regressive psychotherapeutics traces a behaviour pattern back to the original emotion-laden event and then tries to discover the present-day triggering mechanisms that are keeping the past very much alive – a task often complicated by the changing form of the triggering mechanism.

One case exemplifies this point particularly well. A man in his middle twenties came to me with chronic indigestion. His physician had examined him thoroughly and run numerous tests, but found nothing. Dick was concerned about the increasing quantities of medications he was taking, especially since they gave him little relief. After analyzing his eating habits and his way of life, I became convinced that some event of the past must have generated this two-year-old problem.

During the regression the mystery was solved. Dick recalled a life in Sweden during the early eighteenth century in which he lived on a farm with his parents and two younger brothers. Life was demanding. In fact, the only real joy in that life was his befriending of the farm animals, some of which he named and made special pets. One evening Dick came to the dinner table just in time to hear his brother talking about eating the pet rabbit. Dick left the room in tears, but his stern father ordered him back to the table and forced him to eat the rabbit before he could be dismissed. For the remainder of that short life – he died in an accident five years later – Dick avoided eating any form of meat whenever he could get away with it.

The connection to Dick's present indigestion was obvious, especially when he realized that the indigestion first occurred after a Christmas visit with his aunt and uncle on their farm in Indiana. Dick's regression was one of the atypical ones where the past-life trauma was relieved in two hours. For Dick it seemed truly miraculous that he no longer had the slightest stomach pain after eating. For me, it was a reaffirmation of the basic concept of regressive therapy: Relive the past to get it out of the way, so that the present is a richer, fuller experience.

Indigestion is more often than not related to poor eating habits or the stress of this lifetime, but there are diseases and other ailments that often relate to the past. These include, but are not limited to, the following:

1. Allergies
2. Headaches (migraines, especially)
3. Back problems
4. Chronic pain
5. Slow recovery after surgery

Of the mental disorders, depression, suicidal tendencies, and multiple personalities, along with certain other forms of schizophrenia, seem in some cases to be past-life related.

Eighteen-year-old Sandy said she woke up in the night hearing another voice coming from herself. In school she was always wanting to go to a different classroom from her own. Sandy hated her name, though she could give no other. Her mother described her as two different people. One day she was a loving, gentle and intelligent student who wanted to become a veterinarian; the next she was an angry and rebellious motorcycle gang member who engaged in shoplifting. This duality was explained away by her father, who said she was a Gemini, but he was obviously very frightened by his daughter's strange behaviour. Her mother told me that even as a baby Sandy seemed odd, being allergic to certain foods one week and not the next.

Fortunately for Sandy, on the day of her court appearance for the shoplifting, the lovely, gentle person emerged to make a good impression on the judge, and she was given a suspended sentence. Her relieved parents immediately brought her to the Alternative Therapies Council for regression therapy.

Sandy expressed great anger towards her parents in this life, though there seemed to be little basis for it. The reason became clear, however, with her first regression. Sandy was a young girl in a concentration camp, and her present parents were German SS officers. After experiencing the degradation and horror of life in the camp, she went to the gas chamber, where she vividly recalled slowly dying on the floor of the chamber. Sandy was the last to die, having heard the pleas, screams and prayers of those dying around her.

In another series of regressions, Sandy was a tribal chief in a primitive society. It was a life of peace and plenty, and the (male) chief was respected and loved for his wise guidance and strong leadership.

Here is an example of two very different energies of the past that were still alive and warring with each other in the subconscious of a very sensitive young woman. After about a dozen sessions, Sandy came to accept and release the negative energy. When she had done so, the extremes of her behaviour diminished and she was a well-integrated person for the first time in this life.

Illness is not always a simple past-life repression of some emotional pain that refuses to be subjugated any longer. Other reasons for disease that are related to past-life conditions as well as to the needs of the Greater Self (Soul) include:

1. General lack of empathy for others in past lives; bigotry
2. Unwillingness to help others who were debilitated by disease in a past life
3. Unwillingness to develop creative potentialities that are struggling to be expressed
4. Conflicting energies of many past selves that interfere with present-self focus
5. A strongly negative past self trying to live again emotionally in this time frame (negativity is a breeding ground for illness)
6. A specific affliction or impairment from the past that is influencing the present self; a direct carryover.

Dolph, a thirty-two-year-old man, came to me because he wanted to be a runner but he could not get beyond the pain when he ran. Though there was no medical basis for it, the more he ran the more problems he had with his legs. He regressed quickly to the year 1837 and a past life as a sailor on a New England whaling ship. The opening scene found him standing on the dock watching the oil and blubber being unloaded from the ship on which he had served. He was waiting to see what his cut of the profits would be. Dolph seemed inclined to chat with me while he waited.

*   *   *   *   *   *

You hope to be paid $200?

Yes, but it's unlikely. The price is down, I hear.

How much time will that pay cover?

Two years, four months, and nine days . . . no, ten days.

You were gone from home all that time?

Yes, and glad of it. But it does feel good to be back to fresh food I can chew. Had some teeth problems lately.

How old are you?

Twenty-six.

When you are at home, with whom do you live?

My mother [sigh].

What's wrong?

She never wants me to go to sea, even with this kind of money. She wants me to stay at home and wait on her.

Why is that?

She thinks I'm her servant. Do this, do that . . . I get fed up. It makes you want to get away.

Why do you live with her if you don't like her orders?

I promised my father when he died I'd stay with her. But I never said nothing about going to sea in between.

Can you tell me more about your mother?

Ain't much more to tell. She can't walk. She's fat and can't walk and she likes to tell people what to do.

Does she have any friends to help her out?

Nobody can stand her.

Let's go ahead in time several hours, so that you can go home to your mother.

I get . . .

What is it?

The house is empty. Someone is coming up the front walk – I can hear the leaves crunching.

Your mother isn't there?

No. It's the neighbour. She says my mother died in the spring. Well, the house is mine now. I won't have to put up with her no more.

*   *   *   *   *   *

Dolph's complete lack of empathy for his crippled mother was in conflict with his feeling of obligation to fulfill his promise to his father, and it was a conflict that he never resolved in that lifetime. It stayed submerged until Dolph tried to become a runner, and then it manifested in no uncertain terms by pain in his legs. Only after thoroughly examining all the aspects of his conflicted feelings did Dolph begin to relinquish the pain.

Though the karmic connection seems quite obvious in some of these past-life conditions, we must always remember that there is no outside agency deciding our punishment or reward, or determining what we must carry from one life to the next. Before each lifetime, and during it as well, we are always in charge, and we alone decide when certain behaviours are no longer relevant.

In fact, each of us has a responsibility to release those aspects of the past that hinder focus on our present phase of personal growth. We do not want distractions, and the negativities of past lives are nothing more than that. We are healthy by nature and injuries and disease merely reflect the state of the Soul. When we are focused positively on the Now Moment, the Soul is at ease and so is the body.

THE SHACKLES OF FEAR

≈

We never know how high we are
Till we are called to rise;
And then, if we are true to plan,
Our statures touch the skies.

The heroism we recite
Would be a daily thing,
Did not ourselves the cubits warp
For fear to be a king.

EMILY DICKINSON,
WE NEVER KNOW HOW HIGH

If someone were to throw a knife at you, your reaction would be instantaneous and decisive. You would not pause to admire its trajectory or ponder its exact point of impact, but would dodge hastily out of its path. Now, what if the object coming toward you were a tennis ball? For most people, an entirely different response would follow. Recall, however, the case of Linda presented in Chapter 1; Linda was indiscriminately afraid of all flying objects. We consider the fear of a knife to be a rational fear, but Linda's fear of a tennis ball is irrational. Where do irrational fears come from?

Survival is the most fundamental need of every living creature. In common with our fellow creatures, we human beings carry in our genetic coding the ability to recognize danger and deal with it effectively. This coding, which we usually call instinct, leads us to satisfy thirst and hunger, to find shelter, and to reproduce; it also sends urgent signals to our brains whenever any threat to these activities, or to life itself occurs. These signals trigger the emotion of fear, which leads us to take whatever action will get us out of jeopardy.

But humans differ from the other species in some very important ways, including self-awareness and the ability to think abstractly. This leads us to experience fear of *potential* dangers, based on recollections of the past or projections about the future (though even future-related fears are products of the past). Since these fears are nearly always out of proportion to the situations actually encountered, we consider them to be irrational.

Imagine standing on the edge of a high cliff. Your genetic coding will prevent you from walking off the edge – there is no need for you to learn that from experience. If someone standing at your side threatens to push you over the edge, you will respond with real, rational fear, provided that you believe the person means to carry out the threat. However, if just the thought of standing near the edge brings on symptoms of panic, you are experiencing irrational fear.

All irrational fears are learned. Possibly a book or a film dramatized the trauma of a fall from a high place; a childhood friend may have broken a limb in a fall; your mother may have suffered a bad fall while carrying you. It is also very possible that the fear originates in a past life.

Most of the dangers we face today have little to do with physical survival; instead, they are threats to ego survival. When we stop to analyze them, they defy explanation or understanding, yet they are seriously debilitating. Just as though our very life were in danger, such fears cause the hands to sweat, the stomach to churn, the knees to shake; the desire to take action becomes overwhelming. They may be irrational, but they are very, very real.

Psychologists have found their greatest challenge in resolving the various manifestations of fear. Strictly speaking, *fear* is a response to a specific calamity or danger, whether present or in the future; a *phobia* is a horror or aversion of a morbid character; and *anxiety* is uneasiness or generalized fear about uncertain events. Generally speaking, when the fear is obsessive and severely limiting we use the word *phobia*, and when it is generalized and nonspecific we call it *anxiety*.

In counselling, most people come to realize that even a single trauma occurring at some time in their past could have planted the seeds of fear that may bloom in the future. It is the job of the past-life counsellor to uncover that initial trauma. The origins of some fears are evasive (usually, for example, it is a physical fear that brings someone to therapy, though ego survival may be the real issue) and much searching is required to get at their roots. Hypnosis has proved an invaluable tool in the pursuit of this goal.

James came to me because he was handicapped by two fears – of water, and of horses. In regression he had no trouble recalling a lifetime in which he had drowned as a little child. Looking at the scene from the moment just after his death, he watches his mother's frantic attempt to save him.

'My mother is running along the side of the river, trying to grab my leg, but she can't reach me. I'm looking down, as if from a tree, and now I see her trying to run through the water, but the water won't let her get to me. I can see my body in the water and my mother all wet to her waist. She is taking me out of the water and she is crying.'

During the same session, though in a later lifetime, I asked James if he had ever ridden a horse. He said no, and when I asked him if he would like to, he said no again. 'I'm afraid of horses', he said with finality, and changed the subject. The fear of horses was rooted much farther in the past and it would be many sessions later before we uncovered its genesis.

Fear of water is, of course, fairly common, and frequently people with this fear have never learned to swim, which only serves to increase the fear. In Chapter 1 we found that Jean's fear of water derived from witnessing the collision and sinking of two ships in the harbour of an English seaside town. Another client with this fear discovered an even more personal experience at the heart of it.

When Gary had become deeply relaxed he told me that two scenes, both ocean battles, appeared to him. I told him to go with one of them.

'I'm in the water. My arm is cut off and I'm drowning. In the battle

I went through the hull of the ship and over the side. A sharp piece of wood cut through my arm below the elbow. The ship hits me and I go down. I try to keep myself up but I'm losing blood and the water is red. They are too busy fighting to worry about me. I keep hollering but they can't hear anyway with the cannons and the rigging.

'I don't want to die. I don't even have a wife yet. I don't want to drown.'

'What is your name?'

'E. J. Johnson. I'm from the colonies . . . New Jersey. Been at sea about six months. We've been chasing British supply ships. We caught and plundered three of them, but then our sister ship was baited into this trap and these ships came down on us. They are better armed and better trained, but we'll give the British a fight to remember!

'But I won't . . . it's too late for me. All for what? All for what?'

Gary interrupts the anguish of E. J. Johnson to say that he has another scene coming in.

'I am a centurion of the Empire of Rome. There is trouble abroad. We march northward through the forests of Gaul to fight the barbarians. They have no chance against us with our superior weapons and armour. We're invincible and return home victorious, I to my wife.

'Now I must march south. We board war galleys for Sicily and then further south to Africa . . . Carthage. We are going to fight again and we will win. We always win. We go ashore . . . we are ambushed, and I am captured. Oh, NO! I am put in chains . . . how humiliating. Roman soldiers failing! Unpardonable.

'I am in a galley, chained to an oar. We are drawing into battle with many ships. They take our chains off and we are forced to fight because they are too close. Just as I am about to jump from the galley to the next ship I get a blow to the shoulder and fall into the water between the two ships. I'm still alive, but I am being crushed between the two ships. God, I'm drowning. I don't want to drown . . . not again. I open my mouth and move down to end it as fast as possible. Oh, water in the lungs is horrible. I must do it fast; no need

THE SHACKLES OF FEAR ~

to suffer more. Looking down, I see my body floating. It has died.'

In both of these lifetimes Gary spoke of loved ones and returning to them during life and again just after dying. He almost seemed to have learned techniques for drowning as easily as possible, but he carried the horror of it from life to life, and it is no wonder that he feared water in this present life.

A stimulation of any one of the scenes, or a combination of them, can trigger a memory that is associated with fear. A traumatic memory called up by the smell of roses can release an anxiety seemingly unrelated to flowers, or even initiate an irrational fear of flowers. The sound of a train whistle may arouse great inner turmoil. The touch of a silk garment or the taste of lemons may reopen the wounds of the past.

One elderly man came to me a few years ago with the sound of a popular song running through his mind. It just would not go away. Day and night, no matter what he was doing, the same refrain played in his mind, until at last he decided to seek help. In regression the man, whom we will call Jackson, returned to a life as a concert pianist in mid-nineteenth century Germany. His favourite piece, and the one he performed most often, was Mozart's Piano Concerto No.22 in E flat. There is a haunting similarity between the contemporary song and the Mozart piece, but the connection was much more than that.

In that lifetime Jackson had a vile temper, and his wife was a constant drain on his creativity, never recognizing his creative talents or his need to work. One particular day she had interrupted his practising repeatedly. That evening she did it once more as he was playing the Mozart, and he sprang from the piano bench and strangled her to death. From then until the present Jackson's fear of being accused of her murder was attached to the Mozart concerto – or to anything that suggested it.

A place, a name, a date, a word, or a person can trigger fear if the original connection has been made under severe stress. Many individuals have brought to me their fears of heights, insects, darkness, or whatever, hoping that they may uncover a past-life connection. Very often they do.

Reggie came for a regression because of the rather common fear of snakes. In his case, however, the fear was so great that it seriously hampered his ability to function. The scene opened for him in a cave that was nearly pitch black. As a pretty, black-haired girl of seventeen, he stood barefooted in the midst of hundreds of poisonous snakes. The girl had been chosen by her people to be sacrificed to the gods. Though she was terrified, there was no one to whom she could turn for rescue. Within seconds, snakes had bitten the girl and she lay down to die. Interestingly, when asked if her sacrifice had pleased the gods, she said yes.

We all know how fear limits life, distracting us from other pursuits and preventing us from responding positively in so many situations. Whether it is fear of water or of flying objects, of failure or of success, we are thwarted from taking the risks that are so necessary for growth. The fear of rejection and disapproval binds many people to old patterns that seem safe even though they are painful.

Freud believed that all phobias were created by us to mask even more dreadful fears, all of which related to unresolved oedipal feelings. Such an interpretation is too restrictive, for we can find many reasons for fears, only some of which are related to parental relationships. It is true that some fears are created to avoid involvement or to escape risk, but even such a tactic must be traceable to an incident where the individual learned to avoid something at all cost.

Some people use their fears to manipulate others, wearing them like badges of honour to garner attention and protection. For most of us, however, there is a strong desire to let go of fear – to work it out and be free. Sometimes a single regression will turn up the causative event, while for others a combination of therapeutic methods and patient work over a number of sessions is required.

The following list presents some of the common fears that can be dissolved through past-life regression. It is representative, but by no means complete.

| acrophobia | heights |
| ailurophobia | cats |

aictiophobia	sharp, pointed objects
algophobia	pain
androphobia	men
anthophobia	flowers
anthrophobia	other people
apiphobia	bees
aquaphobia	water
autophobia	aloneness, isolation
aviaphobia	flying
belopophobia	needles
brontophobia	thunder
catagetophobia	ridicule
coitophobia	sexual intercourse
claustrophobia	closed spaces
cynophobia	dogs
entomophobia	insects
equinophobia	horses
gynephobia	women
hemartophobia	making a mistake
herpetophobia	lizards, reptiles, crawling things
melissophobia	bees
mysophobia	dirt, germs
necrophobia	death
nycotophobia	darkness
ochlophobia	crowds
ophidiophobia	snakes
pathophobia	illness
pyrophobia	fire
sitophobia	eating
taphophobia	being buried alive
thanatophobia	death
xenophobia	strangers
zoophobia	animals

The structured hypnotic session has proven to be very effective in dealing with such fears. For most people this will include two elements – regression to the causative incident and behaviour modification to learn new patterns of response to the triggering mechanism. Generally the irrational aspect of the fear must be acknowledged and rejected. A small minority of people are released from their fears with the regression alone. In the unusual case of Helen, the grieving widow of Chapter 1, it was not even necessary to get to the roots of her problem, release from negativity and self-limitation coming about simply through recalling a happy, carefree earlier existence.

Regressions often call up scenes from primitive cultures, which implies that fears within us are frequently of ancient origin. Alice had always had a phobia that prevents her from driving under bridges, hill walking, and even from climbing a ladder. In her regression, Alice recalled a scene where she was part of a sacrificial ceremony. She was being ordered by a tribal chief to jump off a cliff.

The regression experience was not easy for Alice, and she avoided the edge as long as she possibly could. When she finally did step off, she was not aware of falling sensations. Avoiding mention of the trauma of the fall and the impact of the rocks below, she seemed quite blasé in her description of the body on the rocks. Since she was apparently unable, even in regression, to confront her terrifying experience, I felt that Alice would be back many more times to work on her fear of heights. However, several weeks later I received the following letter:

Regression of Nov. 22, 1978

Prior to the regression I recall *no* fear, really not even expectancy, as we weren't sure I would regress in that particular session. Being my first experience, I had nothing to anticipate, anyway. I just felt relaxed, trusting and 'open'.

On the cliff I felt no conscious fear, even as the edge approached. Just extreme discomfort, bewilderment and cold. I don't recall actually going over and at no time did I feel the sickening sensation of falling and panic that I had always felt or anticipated when on or looking up to a high place. I recall no sensation of hitting the ground, no pain, nothing. I just went from the very edge into a floating sensation of darkness (a very short sensation) and then a really *beautiful* feeling of being – not floating really, just *there* – in a beautiful light and warmth. I think the best way to describe it might be like being held up but without any sensation of a body or feeling pressure from the holding. The feeling almost defies description. The colours surrounding me were primarily beautiful shadings of gold and pink, but the greatest impression was of just light and warmth. I felt totally detached, emotionally as well as physically, from the body of the young girl at the foot of the cliff. I don't recall being aware of hearing any music.

When I walked out onto the Golden Gate Bridge, 4 days after the regression I *knew* I could do it! I felt free and happy! I did not look down on the section with open railing, but walked over close to the railing, close enough to touch it. Cars and trucks were rumbling by and even though there was movement I felt no fear, no sickness. Just a deep freedom. At the section with solid concrete I leaned way over and looked directly down. Again, no fear. I anticipate walking out considerably farther soon.

A big plus from the death experience is that I seem, since the regression, to 'see' people differently. I believe that it is an awareness – a *real* awareness – of the immortality of their Being; of how precious each is. I have felt very open emotionally and very tranquil since the experience.

An interesting thing happens when people decide to do whatever is necessary to overcome a physical fear. The resolve to conquer the fear entails taking what seems at the time to be an enormous risk, but the determined person forges onward and is successful. Looking back, he or she realizes that there was really little or no risk involved. This is a discovery of tremendous significance.

Even more important is the reclaiming of personal power that takes place as the fear is released. Having let go of a physical fear and emerged stronger and happier – in short, having lost nothing of value – enables a person to risk letting go of less tangible fears. Threats to ego survival cause less resistance and less stress in people who have rejected helplessness and reclaimed their power.

No Man is an Island

≈

> *No man is an island, entire of itself; every man is a piece of the Continent, a part of the main; if a clod be washed away by the sea, Europe is the less, as well as any promontory were, as well as if a manor of thy friends or of thine own were; any man's death diminishes me, because I am involved in mankind; and therefore never send to know for whom the bell tolls; it tolls for thee.*
>
> JOHN DONNE, *DEVOTIONS*

At the age of three, Steven spoke several times of being in the garden, though his family had no garden and no idea of what he meant. Gradually he stopped talking about it. When Steven was eight his mother, a calm and open woman, brought him to me for counselling. He had become hyperactive and was having problems with bedwetting, sleepwalking, and nightmares.

Although hyperactivity can be caused by a number of factors, including inconsistent discipline, reactions to foods and food additives, and even drug reactions, many cases seem to be related to the influence of past lives. More specifically, the personal relationships of the present trigger memories that cause the hyperactive behaviour. Because Steven showed such a complex anxiety response, I felt his difficulties were probably rooted in the past.

Children are very receptive to hypnosis, since they have not built walls of suspicion and fear, and I have had much success in using past-life regressions to reduce or eliminate hyperactivity. I was not surprised that after only a brief induction Steven's facial muscles relaxed, his breathing slowed, and his whole body looked limp.

I asked him to pretend that he was travelling in a time machine into the past, his own past, and suggested that he would be able to feel that he was really in the scene as it unfolded around him. Steven readily spoke about the events of his birth, mentioning how cold the world felt when he entered it and how noisy everything seemed. He complained about the bright lights and rough handling but, since his comments were quite common, I did not feel that his birth was different enough to produce the trauma that was triggering his present behaviour.

I asked Steven to get back into his time machine and travel to a more distant time and place, when he had had a different body entirely and people may have looked and spoken differently. His next stop proved to be in the Scottish countryside.

'Something is wrong with me', Steven said slowly with a scowl. 'I feel all bent up. But the garden is pretty and it smells so good out here.' I wanted to know what it smelled like indoors.

'It smells like leather', said Steven. 'Leather, and all the stuff that goes on it to make it last.'

Steven's father was a tanner who also made leather garments and riding gear. The garden was outside the shop he shared with a cloth merchant. When I asked the name of the place it sounded like 'Killing' and I asked who was killing whom.

'No! *Killin*', Steven corrected me. 'Killin on the loch.' His speech had modulated into a Scottish burr. It seemed unlikely that an American eight-year-old would know the word *loch*, so I asked what it was.

'It's water. We're on the edge of it. It's nice in summer but terrible in winter. There are no flowers then.'

The flowers were obviously important to Steven in the past incarnation, providing him with comfort and beauty in what was revealed to be a limited and dreary existence. Day after day he sat alone in the garden, carried there by his father. In winter his world was the stuffy, chemical-laden atmosphere of the tannery. The family lived behind the shop in very crowded quarters, but the conflicts among them produced a high degree of emotional isolation. Unlike the others, Steven had no means of escape from this setting because of his physical incapacity. Asked about each family member individually, he invariably commented that they ignored him because he was such a burden when there was so much work to be done.

Guided back to a fully conscious state, Steven still had a faraway look in his eyes when he said, 'My mother was my father. My father was my sister. That's weird!'

'Why do you say that, Steven?'

A puzzled look came over his face. Obviously he had no framework in which he could fit the information comfortably. But Steven had glimpsed the past and, in so doing, had answered the most pressing questions about his present life. My recommendations to his mother were simple: surround Steven with plants and flowers, encourage his independence, and give him an abundance of love and attention. Interestingly, when Steven's mother heard the tape of her son's regression, she said in amazement 'I have always had a very peculiar feeling when I smelled leather.' She recognized that she tended to be both over-protective and irrationally impatient with her son, both of which were clearly hold-overs from their previous relationship.

One month later Steven was a changed person. In fact, he had taken such an interest in plants that he was reading everything he could find on the subject. The hyperactivity had faded away.

It is safe to say that all of us are influenced both positively and negatively by our past-life relationships. Since we are at all times the sum of everything we have ever experienced, there is no denying the effect on us of those relationships, though we seldom become aware of them through our conscious minds, which tend to focus on only one reality at a time. The metaphysical principles of relatedness and attraction ensure that relationships never end, though they may be continually changed and modified. Relationships are forever.

How do relationships begin in the first place? Initially they are created to satisfy a physical or a psychological need. Our thoughts today create the relationships of tomorrow. Often a relationship on a higher level is not so much filling a need as reflecting what we are. Thus relationships come into being and evolve along various lines according to our changing needs and evolving personalities.

We are changing all the time, and many relationships in the present life are new. We feel the newness of these affiliations; we feel the building of some and the ebbing of others. But a certain percentage of current relationships are old – some very old and still evolving.

Josh and Jason are identical twins, so much alike that even those who know them well have great difficulty in distinguishing between them. In separate regressions, with no awareness of what the other recalled, the twins revealed many past lives together and corroborated the details of each other's recollections. They raised camels together in the African desert; they worked side by side as carpenters in the early Christian Era; they herded flocks across the barren tundra of Asia; they hid from the invading armies of Napoleon; and they crossed the American plains in search of fertile land. Through more than two dozen lifetimes they intertwined in various roles as mother and son, mother and daughter, and most often as brothers. In one lifetime they were teacher and student in ancient Rome. Time and time again their energies drew them together to fulfill basic growth needs, providing each other with opportunities to expand and adapt more fully to the challenges of the Earth plane.

Two souls may cycle through many kinds of relationships as they meet in one life after another. Among the wide variety of possibilities the two may express their connection in any or all of the following ways:

1. Parent/child
2. Siblings
3. Lovers
4. Relatives
5. Business associates
6. Teacher/student
7. Marriage partners

When such an ancient relationship exists, the persons involved may be very strongly attracted or they may be antagonistic, but they will never feel neutral towards one another. They may, in fact, be both attracted and repelled, which can lead to feelings of great confusion. The married couple who were the first people I regressed to a past life had a very strong desire to be together but carried through many lifetimes and into the present the rivalries of their life as scientists in Atlantis as an impediment to their present happiness.

In another case of intense but confused feelings a thirty-six-year-old woman client described the strong bond of affection between her and one of her sons; though there was a deep inner rapport felt by both of them, he was extremely rebellious and she felt unbearable guilt whenever she disciplined him.

The woman regressed to a life of a male slave labourer who was helping to build a gigantic, underground prison near Cairo. This man, seventy years old and with the gnarled hands of a blacksmith, was part of a 'chain' gang of men roped together round their waists in order to drag huge boulders across the ground and tumble them down a sort of mine shaft where they could be used in shoring up the underground structure. Though he was a slave, the man was filled with memories and shame to be part of constructing what he referred to as 'that godawful secret city of evil, a sewer for people.'

'Do you know anyone in that prison?' I asked. A look of great pain came over 'his' face.

'My older brother Isaac is down there. I wish he would die. I don't know how he has lived so long like that . . . it's a sort of defiance, I guess. It's a terrible burden to see him.'

'How did he come to be there?'

'We were caught up in a drunken street brawl, and he killed a government official who was attacking me. If he hadn't done it I would be dead.'

'And you have felt indebted to him ever since?'

'Yes. Somehow I know it is important that he be able to see me. I don't know why he keeps on struggling. When he dies, I will die. I hope it is soon.'

After the regression, my client told me that she recognized the older brother as her son in this lifetime, and it was easy to understand the guilt feelings and rebelliousness that often came between them.

Past-life regressions help us to realize that we experience lifetimes with particular people as often as we wish. Sometimes it may be a few select individuals and other times it may be a larger group with some underlying purpose or direction. Often there is one individual with whom we have unfinished business.

Beth came to me originally for help in losing weight, and we set up a nutritional programme designed to handle that aspect of the problem while agreeing to explore past lives for clues to the original cause of her weight gain. The scene opened for Beth as she sat in the pew of a little white Methodist church.

'My name is Sarah and I'm fifteen years old. Jonathan is in front of me. He turns to watch me out of the corner of his eyes. He's seventeen. He has broad shoulders, is wearing a rough cotton shirt and boots. He just watches me and I blush. He has a nice smile. He is so beautiful.'

'What is your birthdate, Sarah?'

'June 2, 1742. Such beautiful blue eyes . . .' I interrupt the preoccupied young lady and asked her to move ahead in time to the day of her marriage.

'We are outside under the trees, and my little sister just gave me some flowers. Jonathan put his arms around me. He looks so funny with his suit . . . the collar is big in the back. He looks silly but beautiful. I'm so happy. The ceremony is over now and we are in the wagon, going to some place. Those broad shoulders look so good . . .'

'Sarah, go ahead a year and tell me about your life.'

'I don't think he loves me as much as I love him. He always seems to be thinking about someone else. He works a lot in the fields, even after dark – at least, that's what he says. He turns away from me in bed. I don't know what to do. I'm going to have his baby and he's excited about the baby but not about me.'

'Go to the birth of the baby', I suggested. [Beth began to cry uncontrollably.]

'He's leaving . . . he's just walking away. He wanted the baby so bad, but our son died only a few days after he was born.' [Much crying.] Jonathan's found somebody else, but he won't talk to me. He's so cold. I'm calling to him, holding out my arms, but he's just walking away from the clearing, and I'll never see him again. Oh, Jonathan, what will I ever do without you?'

'You are getting old, Sarah', I tell her. The crying finally ceases.

'He never came back. I'm all alone. Every day is like the one before. Now I'm forty-seven and I'm dying. My knee gave out and I can't stand up. I'm trying to pull myself along the ground to get inside. I just want to see him one more time. I'm starving, but I'm too weak to eat, anyway. How much I want death. I can't feel my legs any more. Some of me is floating . . . nothing matters any more . . . the pain is going away. It's bright, so bright. My sadness for Jonathan has dissolved. I still don't know why he left me but it's all right now.'

'As a Soul entity, do you wish to look over all the lives you have lived to find others shared with Jonathan?'

'In Greece, I was male and he was female. In Egypt, I was male again, and we were both healers, working together. In Atlantis I was female, he was male – an engineer working with something very technical that I didn't understand, something to do with light. We were lovers, always together, he was Aram and I was Alana. We were together before that but there is so much space I can't see it.'

A few weeks after this touching regression experience, Beth phoned me to tell me what had just happened to her.

'As you know, I attended a conference this past weekend', she began. 'There was a period of meditation during yesterday's session, and my mind returned to the anguish I had felt as Jonathan was leaving me. My mind was saying "Jonathan, come back, come back" and all the sadness was rising to the surface as it had during the session. After the meditation period the group took a break, and more than a hundred people were milling around me, but I was still in my own world. Then someone spoke to me.

'I looked up to see a beautiful man looking down at me. He said "I was sitting on the far side of the room before the break. I don't know why, but I felt I had to come over to you as soon as possible." It was Jonathan.'

In all cases where we come together again with people from past lifetimes, the decision is ours. Regression has made this clear: *we decide, and it is a mutual decision.* It is also clear that relationships continue without physical embodiment in a non-time existence as we experience other portions of the multi-dimensional self. Those who have explored relationship regressions come to one inescapable conclusion: *separation is an illusion.*

When we realize that our senses often give us distorted and limited concepts of reality, we open ourselves to the knowledge that we are more than a physical body, that there is an eternal quality to all of us that intertwines with the eternal quality of others. The eternal Self evolves and grows through various time periods and various environments with the need for others always strongly felt.

Relationships are energy harmonies and disharmonies. If we think how problem relationships have helped us to grow as much as the pleasurable ones have, it is easy to understand that relationships are energy interactions. Some are harmonious and others are full of challenge and discord. We feel this truth if we get in touch with the non-physical elements of our being.

Annie came to the Alternative Therapies Council because she was caught up in a love–hate triangle with her husband Jeff and their six-year-old daughter Jody. The three of them were entangled in a web of jealousy, expectation, and disappointment that made all of them thoroughly miserable. In her regression, Annie found herself a saloon girl in a small town in Kansas. Her name was Marie Sullivan and the date was 14 March 1849.

Marie is upset because her youngest sister, Amy, is upstairs with the saloon owner, Robert McCullough. (It later becomes clear that Amy is the present-day daughter Jody, and Robert is the present husband, Jeff).

'How do the three of you get along?' I asked Marie.

'Not too well right now. This is a lousy life and Amy is getting pulled into it. Robert is making it look glamorous and pleasurable, better than it really is. Being a bar girl is degrading. It's bad enough that I have to do it. Amy thinks she is in love with Robert and I can't get through to her.'

'How old is Amy?'

'She's fourteen and Robert's twenty-seven. He doesn't really care about her, just pretends to so that she'll work here. I want to go up there, but I'm afraid of what I might walk into.'

'Have you been in love with Robert?'

'I loved him at the beginning and I thought he loved me. But I've seen too many women come and go through this place and I know Amy's just another woman to him.'

Suddenly moved to action, Marie takes a bottle upstairs with her. A fight ensues when she hits Robert with the bottle and he beats her, but Amy thinks the whole thing is Marie's fault. In despair, Marie leaves Kansas and eventually makes it across the country to San Francisco, where she gets a job in a bakery. She writes to Amy, but get few replies. Marie marries a man named Michael.

Then Amy becomes pregnant, and goes to join Marie in San Francisco. When the baby is born Amy gives it to her sister and brother-in-law.

'Did you ever hear what happened to Robert?' I asked.

'No, and I could not care less', said Marie with finality.

Now, in their present lifetime as a family, these three people are taking another opportunity to work out their relationships satisfactorily. The clues from Annie's regression have provided some insights which they can incorporate into the process.

For each of us, at the most personal level, the multitudes of our past lives interact with each other, causing us to be multiple-relationship personalities. All the past selves and the ways they act and react to one another create the present-focus personality. This is in addition to the relationships we have with *other* individuals as we travel through incarnations, and in addition to the group dynamics that occur in various clusters of personalities with whom we travel.

On the largest scale, we realize that nations relate to nations in peace and in war based upon past experience together in different time frames. Thus the relationships that we are part of at all times are not just the simple one-to-one, person-to-person involvements, but extend from the many selves that we are to the complex inter-relationships between nations.

A relationship is always established by mutual consent. Figuratively, a contract is written and signed. In very specific ways, we expect the affiliation to satisfy some need that we have, the most important of which is the opportunity for growth. It is personality interactions that help us create our awareness of ourselves. We would like to think that, in various relationships, we are who we think we are, but realistically speaking, we often function as who we think others think we are.

Confrontation is necessary in relationships. For learning and growth to occur, confrontation and challenge must be present in a relation-ship. Most regressions prove this point. Some people, however, carry forward only the emotional trauma of the confrontation without realizing the spiritual lesson that the encounter has provided. It is important in all impasses in relationships, in all difficult times with others, that we seek the spiritual lesson. This neutralizes the nega-tive emotional energy that can be carried like excess baggage from one life to the next.

Failure in relationships is necessary to shock us into awareness and to help us to understand more completely our place in the scheme of things. Just as wrong answers in an examination teach us much more than right answers, poor responses in relationships tell us much – if we see the spiritual message. On the surface, none of us likes to fail at anything, whether it be a test or a marriage.

Past-life regressions help us to see the spiritual message in the relationship that did not work, the energy of which we carried into the present time frame. Being in touch with the initial interaction helps us to see beyond the emotional involvement. No matter whether a relationship of the past is smooth or bumpy, we grow, for all kinds of alliances expand awareness and awareness expands rela-tionships.

Through the challenge that alliances provide, we move closer to unconditional love. For some the process is slow and ponderous, and many encounters with the same people are necessary, while for others the pace is quickened by assimilation of the principles of the encounter. A good relationship cannot be forced to happen. It must evolve through persistent, patient effort, extending most often over a series of lifetimes.

A present relationship that is especially stormy or unusually harmonious is sure to be rooted in the past. Such has been the case with hundreds of clients with whom I have worked specifically on relationships problems. Most often the problem is between husband and wife, but more and more, mothers and fathers are wanting to know why they feel certain ways towards their children, and children are hoping to find out what prevents them from relating more effectively with their parents. More often than not, we are working out old problems in new ways.

Each lifetime provides the conditions that make the working through possible. Unfortunately, most of us are not in touch with this potential for resolutions, and so it is ignored as we compound difficulties and fail to realize avenues for harmony and fulfilment. There is no boring replay of the same scenario from lifetime to lifetime. Although the souls may be the same, the play and scenery changes, and the purpose is modified each time around.

Love at first sight happens because of an awareness of the past. It is an intuition that is totally blind to outward appearances. There is a deep recognition of an earlier contract that worked harmoniously – a time when there was a blending of two energies as one.

Although this concept is usually applied to male–female love relationships, this is not the only kind of relationship where instantaneous reunion is felt. Soul mates, as they are often called, may be individuals in any form of relationship. A brother and sister may be soul mates, or a father and son, niece and aunt, two close friends, and so forth. There need be no sexual aspect to the relationship for it to be of the soul mate level.

The only criteria for soul mates is that they be in tune with each other on all levels, that they consciously and unconsciously meet the needs of each other, and that they communicate without words as much as with words. Soul mates experience a communion of Souls, an elevating blending of energies providing fulfilment and freedom. Each basks the other in the radiance of unconditional love and forgiveness.

Soul mates are two closely aligned energy frequencies broadcasting simultaneously. They have broadcast together through the ages both in physical incarnation and out, and only physical death brings temporary sadness to the one left behind. Even then, the inner knowledge of togetherness transcends the grief of physical separation.

Some people try to predetermine who their soul mate will be and are sure they will recognize the partner according to some list of features. It just does not happen that way. Some people come to counselling to find their soul mate through regression. Sometimes this provides clues, sometimes it creates confusion, but often it emphasizes the fact that the higher dimension of self must be focused to recognize the soul mate when he or she appears.

I have noted a number of development areas that we work in through relationships: they could be called development themes. We concentrate our energies and try to develop proficiency in the area of concern, and often more than one lifetime is required for us to develop mastery of the theme. These themes, which we work on separately and in combination, are:

1. Creative–spiritual development
2. Emotional development
3. Mental development
4. Physical development
5. Sexual development

Although we work on the creative–spiritual aspect to some extent in every lifetime, it is only occasionally the main theme. Relationships provide us with the best opportunity to develop creativity and spirituality, however, whether or not it is the primary theme. The universal law of attraction supports creative–spiritual development, for we pull to us not only those Souls of past incarnations who we know will inspire our uniqueness, but also those who will actively thwart it.

Nothing drives a person on to greater heights with more power than the recognition of barriers and the efforts to overcome them. In fact, one indicator of spiritual evolution is the number of different and widely varied personalities we draw to us. The person who looks around and finds that nearly everyone is identical, is working almost exclusively on one particular development theme. Past-life regressions reveal the patterns we are following and help us to see more clearly the kinds of directions we need to move ourselves consciously. Knowing which theme we are working on gives us the freedom to complete it and move on.

Emotional development seems to be the most prevalent life theme in the world today. It accounts for the great disharmonies between people and nations and points to the immature level on which humankind finds itself. Comparing the growth of humanity to the growth of an individual, we can see the emotionalism and possessiveness that is so representative of early childhood being displayed on a larger scale between individuals and societies. Many hundreds and even thousands of years will be required for us to move into the maturity phase of development, where childish behaviour is replaced with patience and love.

While creative–spiritual development represents the most advanced life theme – as seen in individuals such as Jesus and Buddha – emotional development represents the most basic theme. It is the first to be mastered, requiring many lives for some. Since the universe knows nothing of time there are no timetables for progress along a theme. But, as the Buddhist affirms, everyone, regardless of his or her pace, reaches the sunlit mountain peak. Somehow insight must be gained to hasten an unnecessarily slow climb (by human standards). Past-life regressions provide a tool for this.

Some people are surprised and disappointed when in regression they return to past lives that are little different than those occurring now – lives characterized by jealousy, suspicion, anger, frustration, resentment, and fear. Thus it is the emotional theme that is most often identified in regression, since this is the collective developmental level of humanity from the beginning to the present time.

For this reason, I feel that Souls first incarnate in primitive societies and progress through increasingly complex social structures as they feel ready to develop emotions on a higher level. To date, no one in regression has indicated that the present lifetime is the very first. The majority, in fact, point to at least two dozen previous lives, with the greatest number mentioned being one hundred and seven! Invariably, those first encounters with the Earth plane, whether in the prehistoric past or in recent times, have occurred in undeveloped cultures where emotional expression is generally related to physical survival.

Sometimes a Soul will forgo emotional development in favour of mental development, feeling that a more appropriate set of circumstances for emotional growth will occur further down the road. The cloistered life of Brother Timothy, for instance, centred almost exclusively on mental and spiritual development.

Mental development can sometimes act as an avoidance mechanism – an escape route, so to speak. Often those individuals operate very much like computers, with emotions unrecognized or invalidated, because life experiences have indicated to them that emotional expression is unacceptable. In past incarnations they have interacted with people who have invalidated what little emotional expression they revealed, so survival needs led them to sidestep the emotional from then on.

When mental development through relationships is a survival tool rather than a carefully chosen Soul growth experience, it leads to unhappiness and often solitude. This person finds many people of the past are still trying to invalidate the emotional self. Regression makes this clear, and shows the individual how to work through emotions with these personalities of the past.

The same client, Jack, who lived once as Brother Timothy, recalled a later life with startling similarities, but with the addition of some emotion-laden family relationships. In this late nineteenth-century lifetime he was a minister. He was closely associated with Yale University, about which he said that he was hoping to see them expand their divinity school. A learned and sophisticated man, he was nevertheless sternly moralistic about the behaviour of his family members, and his daughter had just become pregnant out of wedlock.

'There has been a very great backsliding on the part of my oldest daughter. I'm not particularly happy with myself at the present time because I've been very hard on my girl, and both my wife and daughter are really cross at me. But I must be firm. I told her she was on her own with this and she was going to have the baby, but unfortunately the baby died.

'I didn't approve of this fellow she thinks so much of, so I'm still quite beside myself. I don't know what part I could have played in this, but I've tried to be some comfort to her in her bereavement. However, she is just going to have to adjust herself and marry Edgarson. But it has to be her choice; I can't be her conscience any more. I am concerned about her younger sister, who looks up to her so much. I must be honest and admit that I am making judgements from my position in the community . . .'

Jack had come to counselling with the comment that he related better to his mother-in-law than he did to his wife. In this regression, his wayward daughter is now his wife, and the wife then is presently his mother-in-law. Once again, three people have the opportunity to work out their emotional problems together. With each succeeding lifetime there is less opportunity to escape into the mental aspect of life.

A life of physical development will reveal itself as an intense concern for the physical body. Body building, involvement in sports throughout an entire lifetime, or adoption of a career such as modelling are all indicators that this is the theme being emphasized. Even over-dependence on the senses is a sign of emphasis on physical development.

The lover of music may be so stimulated aurally that it signals work on the physical itself. On the other hand, music may be a tool for the development of the emotional or the creative–spiritual self. Regression often reveals the true emphasis.

Regression of people with weight problems reveals difficulty relating to their physical bodies and the tendency to attract others who face the same challenge. Excess weight is a sign that too much attention is being placed on the emotional theme and not enough is focused on the physical. Scenes of food deprivation and starvation in past lives often show the lack of attention to physical needs.

Frequent changing of sexual roles helps us to maintain sexual balance throughout all of our lifetimes. Sexual awareness may be a major theme, however. If this be the case, we will vary roles from life-time to lifetime, being excessively masculine or feminine in one life or a series of lives. We even choose homosexual roles to focus our attention on the balance between masculinity and femininity if we have been identifying too strongly with either one in past lives. Some clients regress to a long series of one-sex roles, an over-emphasis that usually explains why the individual will go to extreme lengths to prove true to that role.

Relationships of the past provide us with six potentials for self-awareness. The people with whom we travel fill the roles of:

1. Mirror: Reflecting an image of who we are and where we are in all the themes of growth, by comparison and contrast.
2. Catalyst: Sparking us in the quest for fulfilment.
3. Guide: Pointing out the way.
4. Ally: Acting as confidant, the person with whom we can be completely ourselves.
5. Provider: The supplier of needs.
6. Teacher: The facilitator of clearer vision.

The way we choose our parents exemplifies all of the preceding rela-tionship possibilities, for we know everything about our prospective parents before we choose them. As Soul beings we are able to 'test the water' before submerging ourselves in it. Regressions have borne out the fact that although all factors – including sex, nationality, environment, genetics, historical circumstances – are considered, relationships are the most important considering in choosing our parents. The need to be with a particular person or group of people is compelling. The choice we make includes the circumstances and relationships that will provide the kind of growth we are seeking.

If we view the Earth plane as the university of growth potentials, we proceed from one class to the next, from one life theme to the next, only as we master the skills of that class. Either we do well and move on, or we repeat the grade with a mixture of new and familiar classmates and teachers. It is we who decide whether to move ourselves or not. Certain actions are sure to hold us back: selfishness, fear, negativity, possessiveness, and the like.

Taking our own life or that of another is sure to detain us right where we are. Committing suicide is like quitting the class before graduation. (In the school of life there are no social promotions, no special cases, no politics of advancement.) It is the individual responsibility that determines the time to move on. Sometimes we can seek help from the non-physical plane, but even with that advice, the final decision is with us – and challenge is the name of the game.

It is not always the parents with whom we wish to live again, but an older brother or sister, a friend of the parents, or even another child yet unborn. The point is, we look for the nearest possible vehicle to what we desire. Of course it is by mutual consent that we make our final determination. Through telepathic communication with parents before entering into the developing foetus, the decision and contract is made. Sometimes, apparently, the need of the parents for a particular Soul is stronger than the desire of the reincarnating Soul, but mutual agreement still makes the compact for birth. No one is ever drawn into incarnation against his or her will, nor do we ever impose ourselves on unwilling parents.

Factors related to the association of these Souls are considered; nationality is a good example. We would not consider being born to

Eskimo parents if being born to Chilean or South African parents were going to provide a better opportunity of being with the right people to work on the chosen theme.

The genetic component is an important consideration. Do we, for example, wish to be a product of a genetic strain that has produced tall people, or people with brown eyes, or heavy people, or light? Do we need to work with high intelligence or low, with healthy, strong bodies or with various degrees of physical impairment? All factors are known and considered, and all are a matter of choice. Nothing is foisted on us.

At first hearing this may seem impossibly complex, but consider for a moment the incredible complexity that produces the spoken word, or the number of operations that are required to walk just one step. We take these physical events for granted because they are well-known to us, but the non-physical are just as real.

Since we are not perfect in all senses as Souls, but rather striving toward God-like perfection, we do make mistakes in our assessments and choices. We may select the wrong person to be with, or make erroneous choices on some other level. During the early months of life, such a realization allows us to leave the body quite easily, much to the grief of parents; we call this decision 'cot death'. Sometimes we allow the prospective mother to take responsibility for the decision and undergo an abortion. The Soul is not destroyed in either case, since energy – especially Soul energy – cannot be destroyed even if the physical manifestation is eliminated. Any broken contract for a relationship, whether it be through abortion or cot death, or by leaving a marriage through divorce, constitutes a mutual agreement at some level of awareness, just as surely as did the establishment of the contract in the first place.

All relationships are entered into and left on a gradual basis. There is no sudden decision, but a lengthy period of time in which the factors are being considered. Birth and death represent two obvious periods when the decision-making process and the weighing of all factors are seen.

Those who have clinically died on operating tables have described the sensations of moving out of the body and then, considering all the factors of leaving, deciding to return to physical form to finish what was started. Entry into the foetus follows the same pattern, sometimes taking many months for the final decision to be made.

Many clients have described phasing in and out of a new body: apparently it is much like the movement in and out of waking and dreaming states. Several individuals have described the process as similar to tuning in a radio station that fades in and out. It seems that a solid commitment to remain in the new body is made only after several months in the body. There is a general tendency of those who are security conscious and materialistic to enter the developing foetus early, and those who are 'free spirits' (creative, philosophical, and intuitive) to enter late in the pregnancy.

At whatever point the Soul impresses itself on the new body, it implants all of its past experiences as well. The new brain has full awareness for a brief period of time of all past situations, but this super-awareness gradually fades as focus on the present reality becomes stronger. The senses are eager to experience everything and parents generally do not encourage fantasy in children – which of course stifles all the old memories, the stuff of which imagination is born.

Being in harmony with all these past levels becomes necessary when we carry strong emotional charges that inhibit full response to the present time frame. In regression these past life traumas are re-encountered and released. Puzzling relationships that may be part of the blocking are recognized and, through creative response in this time frame, those same Souls are instruments of growth rather than barriers to progress. Relationships should always help us to love ourselves better and encourage spiritual, mental, and emotional growth.

Those Souls with whom we customarily travel are known as our Soul units. The Soul units may be composed of only a few entities with whom we grow and experience every phase of reality, but some Soul units are very large. They may be political units, such as national leaders. To say, for instance, that coincidence brought Washington, Jefferson, Franklin, Adams, Hamilton, and the rest of the Founding Fathers together would be naïve.

Perhaps we can see a better example in Concord, Massachusetts in the middle 1800s. The Concord Circle, they called themselves – a small group of literary geniuses responsible for some of the most memorable writings in America.

Emerson, Thoreau, Alcott, and Hawthorne were close in their work and in their personal lives. They often expressed their deep admiration and appreciation for each other, stating time and again that they felt they had been together before. All were strong believers in reincarnation and in the influence of past lives on the present moment. They called their brand of reincarnational thinking *transcendentalism.*

In sports, in religion, in art, in science, in music, we find like minds working together in what seems to be a unified effort towards some goal. Even whole villages sometimes reincarnate together for some mutually agreed-upon purpose. Whatever structure holds a group together in any series of lifetimes, it serves as the framework that allows the creative interplay of various roles in the achieving of some goal important to the members of the group or to humanity at large.

Thus do human relationships form the very fabric of our existence, and provide each of us with the structure and support necessary to the working out of our individual destinies. In truth, no man is an island.

Let Your Light So Shine

≈

Let your light so shine before men,
that they may see your good works, and
glorify your Father which is in heaven.

MATTHEW 5:16

Mutually enhancing relationships with others are possible only when we are in right relationship with ourselves. The term *self-image* is particularly descriptive of this inner relationship because it is the *reflection* of the light referred to in the quotation from Matthew. That is, our self-image consists of a reflection from the physical world as well as a reflection from the non-physical, spiritual realm. When we 'let our light shine', we reveal the connection between our spiritual selves and our ego selves and we acknowledge the connection between ourselves and the things of the world.

According to this definition of self-image, we are not who we think we are, nor are we who others think we are. We are instead the reflected image of every experience with every person and circumstance that we have ever encountered in all our lifetimes and in the world between. As experiences accumulate, the reflection becomes more and more complete. While both environment and genetics are important in the development of personality and self-image, equally important is our connection with our spiritual selves; together – and only together – they give us a clear and valid picture of who we are.

The relationship between self and Self begins to develop from the womb experience of our first physical lifetime because there is communication between our embryonic consciousness and universal consciousness. Like the process of evolution, self-concept progresses as a rudimentary structure, becoming more sophisticated and evolved as we progress through many lifetimes of experiences. The ego is the director of this process – in fact, the ego could be called the DNA molecule of the psychological self.

My Greater Self, from which this material on self-image comes, describes the developing self-image like this: *'It is as though beings begin with tiny squares of reflective surface at some distance from the viewing point. The reflected image grows as experiences accumulate, until a total reflection is achieved. Unfortunately, expectations distort the mirroring surface'*. Unhappiness and a poor self-image result when *'expectations are disappointed and a negative energy field is created. Expectations when out of control, create the most destructive and totally demoralising self-image'*. On the other hand, a positive self-image is created when expectations are satisfied. *'Expectations that are based upon simplicity and are orientated towards self goals, rather than towards goals for others, are the least disappointed and encourage the most healthy self-image.'*

The Greater Self discusses self-image construction in terms of power struggles by stating that *'the gaining or losing of power is a part of this total self-reflection. Power is, in fact, a constant preoccupation of the evolutionary process, for the psychology of self associates survival with power. Each interaction on your earth plane is a power play, a game of sorts, based upon mutual consent, in which a bargaining system is established. Bidding goes on until the power is bought by the highest bidder – that is, the being that shows the greatest willingness to risk. This occurs at the most subtle levels of beinghood, of course.*

'Power is constantly and consistently sought as a prize. Like magnetic fields existing between beings, and between beings and things, and between beings and events (or environments, or circumstances), a natural energy tension is created. This is, in its beginning phase, the natural energy of power as you would perceive it. The bargaining, then, is with this quantity that exists naturally between these two energy sources. The gaining or losing of power is part of this total self-reflection. Beings from experience to experience, from evolutionary phase to evolutionary phase,

accumulate and process all of these multi-dimensional power reflections. The supreme and serene presence of the spiritual Self is always amused by the multitude of masks worn in the assemblance of data for a self-creation. Life IS creation.'

Focusing our attention on the greatest mirror of all allows a more perfect self-creation. *'Man's noblest achievement is to create himself in the likeness of his Creator* [not the other way around, which has been man's custom]. *More correctly, this means the establishment of an unconditionally loving energy self.*

'Beings that are loving unconditionally are not expecting anything of anyone, but are releasing, with blessings, everyone at all times. People need to develop patience before they can help themselves and before they can experience unconditional love, which is predicated on patience. Remember that self-image is produced unevenly, just as evolution proceeds along unpredictable lines (from human perspective). Unevenness in the development of self-image often parallels unevenness in human interaction.' Clearly we can see the importance of patience.

My Greater Self concludes with a directive on achieving a more positive self-image: *'The fastest way to clarify, purify, and rectify a negative self-image is to clean off the reflective surface. Breathe the breath of love on that surface and polish it diligently. I leave you, bestowing upon you richest blessings.'*

The implications are clear. Love the self first, then extend that love to other people, to situations (even the most difficult and seemingly insurmountable), and to conditions of life. Love helps us to clarify a clouded mirror and helps to smooth a distorted one. In others we see ourselves. Even slight changes in the way we perceive ourselves mean that others will reflect a different image in return.

Communicating with higher dimensions of consciousness – our Greater Selves – allows understandings to flow into us that are necessary for the strength and direction so badly needed in our everyday lives. When it is difficult for us to look to God for a mirror of what we wish to be, we can look to those human mirrors that best represent the power and peace of God in man: Jesus, Moses, Buddha, Mohammed, and others.

People who enter counselling to explore their past lives are often surprised and chagrined to find their present situations very similar to those experienced in past lives. Unconditional love – first of self, then of others – is the key to transforming those persistent problem areas into sources of strength and knowledge.

Remember that patience coupled with the lack of expectations allows the flowering of unconditional love. Experiencing that love, we can understand the power plays, dare to take risks, break through barriers of fear, and diligently polish the mirrors of our self-image 'with the breath of love'. The lights that shine as a result of that polishing can truly glorify God and immeasurably enhance the universe of which we all are part.

II

LIVING HISTORY

≈

There is properly no history:
only biography.

RALPH WALDO EMERSON,
ESSAYS: FIRST SERIES, 'HISTORY'

People often tell me that they feel sceptical about past-life regressions because it seems that everyone regresses to a lifetime as a famous person. In fact, as common sense would indicate, most regressions reveal ordinary lives such as those we and our friends are living at present. Many people would like to think that they had been someone prominent in history, but past lives, like present lives, are generally unspectacular. On the other hand, it is hard to imagine anything more dramatic than the unfolding of a series of lifetimes interspersed with periods of existence in the world between.

Many subjects, perhaps 20 per cent, do regress to historical periods that we find particularly significant or interesting in terms of human evolution. Such encounters surprise the typical subject, who has begun the process of regression without direction to any particular time period. In itself, a historically noteworthy regression provides no greater release from the energies of the past than any other regression, but it is fascinating for both subject and hypnotist to witness history from a living perspective. Of most interest are the small details of life that do not find their way into the history books. These curious details add realism and depth, as well as authenticity, to the regression experience.

Through the eyes of clients I have the privilege of viewing the court of Louis IX, the pagan rites of spring in the South Pacific, and life in the Old West as it really was – rather than as Hollywood has portrayed it. Lincoln is more real to me now as a result of the various first hand descriptions and opinions I have heard expressed about him. Life on the Mississippi has been described for me even more fully than Mark Twain did, and Medieval England is as real to me as twentieth-century America.

The cost of goods, the hardships of life, and the joy of small pleasures have made their mark on my clients. After one person regressed to a simple life in seventeenth-century England, he lost all his anger towards present-day inflation; he realized that he is better off now, even with soaring prices, than he was in the 1600s when most items cost only pennies. This conscious comparison of the present to the past helps to alleviate many anxieties of the present, and most people find themselves taking the position that things aren't so bad after all.

It is possible to make some generalizations about regressions to historical periods. Almost everyone recalls a lifetime in a primitive culture as their first-life experience. Some do cite a first-life experience in Atlantis, which, if we are to believe these regressions, was a very highly developed civilization. Though there are exceptions, most people experience one or more lifetimes in each century. Some people seem to specialize in particular cultures or nationalities, but most experience a wide variety. Invariably when the client encounters an exciting period of history – one about which we know a great deal or in which we have special interest – the person is quite blasé and does not recognize the specialness of the event. For clients who are able to achieve a Level 4 or Level 5 regression, there is often an intriguing ability to draw maps and costumes of these interesting eras. The ability to sign one's own past-life name is quite common.

Sometimes when the person has returned to full consciousness, he or she will dispute information that was revealed during regression. For example, a young woman who recalled an English lifetime of the late 1890s referred to the monarch as Victoria. Upon hearing the tape of her regression she commented 'That's funny. I thought the ruler was a king then.' Another subject who relived an experience during the Civil War was embarrassed upon awakening to realize that he had talked about Robert E. Lee in terms of four-letter expletives.

In the cases that follow, the historical period was significantly connected to the problems of the present day. Notice how each client is unconcerned about the impressiveness of the details that go toward the validity of the lifetime. Each one of the cases was experienced in a very natural way with information generally given in response to questions.

A client named Don had just finished telling me of a stimulating and exciting life as a physician in Ancient Greece when I asked him if he had ever lived in the Egyptian culture. His demeanour changed instantly and he informed me sharply that I had chosen an unpleasant lifetime.

I'm sorry. Why was it unpleasant?

It was hard on body and soul. Very laborious, very strenuous.

What did you have to do that was so hard?

I was building a pyramid.

Did it have a name then?

Not then.

How much of it was completed when you were working on it?

About one-third. It seemed labour without a purpose.

How did you get the stones up to that height?

I didn't. I could only see it in the distance.

What did you do?

With ropes we moved stones over rollers like tree trunks. My calloused hands . . . I hated that work.

Why did you do it?

I was a slave.

How many others were helping to move the stones?

About sixty or seventy in the place where I was working.

You had to pull the stones a certain distance and then let someone else pull them?

We had to stay within the camp area.

Did you have shelters?

No, we slept on mats on the ground. We ate roots and bread.

No meat?

Very seldom.

Did you ever get to see the pyramid up close?

No, and I died before it was finished.

Did you die there?

Yes. A stone fell on me.

Were you old or young?

Young.

Did you ever marry?

No.

So that was your whole existence in that lifetime?

Yes.

This regression indicates that at least some of the construction of the pyramids was done in the backbreaking way that seems so incredible to us, but leaves as a mystery how they raised the monstrous stones to the heights required for completion.

* * * * * *

In regression Gary discovered himself to be a friar in Ireland. As the scene opens he is resignedly preparing for yet another Viking invasion. In stream-of-consciousness fashion he tells the story.

'There is a ship on the horizon – a Viking ship – and another. The friars are scurrying about the castle, gathering food, packing the carts. The ship will have to land down shore because there is only cliff here and it is windy and stormy right now. The Vikings will burn us or kill us . . . they are Godless heathens just out to satisfy themselves. We will go inland until they leave. They destroyed this building before and we had to rebuild it. We must escape – we cannot serve God if we are dead. They are after our lead, gold, silver, and food. They will destroy our religion; they have attacked our monasteries along the Scottish and English coast. It has been going on for centuries now.

'I fled once before. They bludgeoned my father to death, but my mother, sister and I escaped on foot. It was in Malarky, a town several weeks north of here. Why does God let this happen to us?

'We stop our moving to pray: "Almighty God in heaven, where art thou? Where are thine angels come forth to help us?" Then we go back to loading the wagons with all that we have. All the writings . . . precious little ink we have . . . we leave the furniture and some food behind. There are about fifty of us friars, pushing and pulling the wagons through the night, heading inland. It is still raining but we keep going, camping under some trees finally for three days.

'Six of us volunteer to go back and see if the invaders have left. There is the monastery, half burnt, smoke rising from it. I guess God sent the rain to keep it from burning completely. We go on to the monastery and find there is pigs' blood everywhere. They hacked up our altar and spread it with pigs' guts. They made a big bonfire in the middle of our church and feasted there.

'We must clean the stench of the Norse out of here. The place reeks inside . . . burned wood and slaughter. We must go outside constantly for breaths of fresh air. Oh, God [gasp], upstairs there are two horses dead, quartered, sliced open. The stench is so bad . . . we must open the windows to drop the horse carcasses out. There is noise outside. No, Daniel, the Vikings have not returned. It is our soldiers.

'In the name of God, what has taken you men so long to come? What has taken the King so long to send you here? A paltry twenty of you come to protect us! Is this the way of our King? We pray for our King so earnestly and he sends us twenty soldiers, five days late. You men will stay and help us clean. You came too late to protect, so now you clean.'

* * * * * *

In a low-key regression, Kathleen discusses her solitary life in Victorian London. She provides a wealth of homely detail as she strolls through Hyde Park.

What are you wearing, Kathleen?

A long dress, green, with long sleeves. It's spring, but the air is brisk today.

Do you have a job?

No, I used to sew in a factory.

Do you live near the Park?

Yes, I have a nice house. I live alone.

Do you have any friends?

Not really. People I know, but not friends. I used to live with Virginia Beacon, who owned my house. I would sometimes sit in the parlour with Virginia and her friends. They were high-bred, not my class, so I would just listen.

What did they talk about?

Mostly politics. Somebody was always angry. Sometimes it was just gossip.

Did they ever mention the names of anyone you remember?

Just the Queen. Victoria.

Do they approve of the queen?

Some do and some don't. She doesn't influence my life much. I'm apart from it all.

Why is that?

I don't have money, so I don't have to worry about losing it. You don't have to worry about losing something you don't have.

Do you know the local shopkeepers?

I know them . . . the butcher is Jonathan Williams. His father was butcher before him.

What meat do you buy?

A little beef, lamb, some chicken.

Do you buy meat by the pound?

By the piece.

What would a chicken cost you?

A whole chicken . . . about 20 pence.

How about a piece of beef?

Depends on whether it's a good piece. [Chuckling] Actually it's been a long while since I had a good piece of beef.

Are you in good health?

Fairly . . . yes, I can get about.

What other shops do you visit?

The sweets shop.

What do you buy there?

Mostly I just look. [Chuckle].

In what direction do you live from Hyde Park?

West, I think . . . Yes, when I walk home I walk into the sun.

How do you spend your time?

Walking, gardening, some knitting, a bit of embroidery. Sometimes I try to make lace.

*   *   *   *   *   *

Meanwhile, on the other side of the Atlantic an untutored young man named Sam comments on affairs of state in the American South of 1861.

Have you ever travelled, Sam?

Not much . . . just to Atlanta.

Where are you now?

I'm sitting in my room. It's built on the side of the Colonel's house. I've got a couch and a small wood stove.

What are you doing?

I'm trying to learn how to read. I have a book.

What is the book?

It's a speller. Mary brought it from school.

Do you know anything about politics, Sam?

I've never heard the word.

Do you know who is President of the United States?

It used to be Lincoln, but the people here wanted something else. They all didn't want Lincoln no more – they have somebody named Jeff.

That's what everyone calls him? Jeff?

People here do. They call him President Jeff.

How do you feel about the situation?

Doesn't make any difference. I see they're fighting.

Who is?

Our people against their people.

What do you mean – our people against their people?

We used to be with President Abraham, or President Lincoln, whatever his name is. Now we are separated, but he thinks he owns us and wants us back and we don't want to let him in, so we have to fight.

So it's because he wants to tell you what to do that you fight?

Yes. What difference does it make to him?

How is it you are not fighting, Sam?

They haven't called me yet. Right now I'm working loading supplies and food for the soldiers. I load the stuff on trains and they take it away.

* * * * * *

In another mid-nineteenth-century regression we enter the scene of an American pioneer, John Simpson. Simpson is a trapper who has come home to find suspicious circumstances; moccasin footprints leading to his cabin door alert him to the presence of Indians, and he retreats a hundred yards to observe. He converses with me while waiting to see what transpires at the cabin.

What do you think is going on?

Not sure. They're probably after my furs.

Are you just going to wait it out?

Yes. My knife is nice and sharp . . . I put it back in my sheath. Door cracks open a bit.

So there is someone inside?

Yes. I have to check my rifle to make sure it's OK.

What are you going to do if they have your furs?

Kill them, I . . .

Have you ever killed an Indian before?

Yes. Self-defence.

Are you a big man, John?

Big enough to handle them. Six one.

You are bigger than the Indians?

Yes, and smarter, too. If they were smart they wouldn't go in my cabin.

What would be taking them so long?

Maybe they know I'm here and are waiting for dark to slip away. Maybe they found my whisky.

You keep some whisky in the cabin?

Oh yes – outside the cove.

Do you have a wife?

No. My wife and two children were killed.

What happened?

We were in a wagon train coming over the Appalachians . . . I was on horseback a couple miles ahead . . . there was an accident . . . the wagon they were in went out of control . . . my children were crushed under it . . . Becky, my wife, had a broken neck from being thrown from the wagon.

Did you bury them right there?

I buried them. People offered to help but it was my job. Took a long time . . . had to stop and cry.

Why had you decided to come West?

Becky and I grew up together in Pennsylvania. All the good land was taken. We were young and wanted to do something different. We knew it was going to be hard, but it would be worth it.

So you continued West after losing your family?

There was nothing for me back home; just old feelings which I could not handle at the time with her being dead.

What possessions do you have, John?

Rifle, knife, clothes on my back, bundle of pelts, gun powder, utensils, a table and chair I made during the winter.

What pelts do you go after?

Beaver and fox; I got about a half dozen bear pelts.

How much do you get for your pelts?

Last year I got about $200. It depends on the market. I have maybe $60 left this spring.

Two hundred dollars goes a long way?

Oh, yes.

What would it cost you for a good meal in town?

All the way back to St Louis?

Could you get a good meal for a dollar?

It better be good for a dollar.

What do you normally eat?

Venison, corn meal for biscuits . . . make a lot of things with flour . . . pancakes for breakfast, wild eggs. Sometimes I get myself some turkey or pheasant for dinner.

Do you experience hunger very much?

Not too much. I'm fairly careful about it. Couple of winters ago I was down on rations and snowed in about two or three hundred miles further up. I rationed the food out so much a day. When I could leave the cabin I went a couple miles and found a pheasant, I ate it half raw . . . plucked it from the fire and ate the outer pieces as they cooked.

Why don't you have a horse?

Too mountainous. Besides, you have to feed a horse, and there's not enough grass for horses . . . The door is opening, there are three Indians . . . funny, they are bare-chested. I raise my rifle.

What are they doing?

Two of them are carrying my pelts and the third has some of my food. I don't want to hit the pelts, but I will risk it if I have to. I fire at the first and hit him in the shoulder . . . shatters it completely. I've laid my pistol out by my hand, all ready. I pick it up – they are only about twenty feet away. They see me, but I've got them first. I fire the pistol and hit the second one in the face. I jump to my feet with my knife and run toward the third Indian. It's hard in the dark, but I know the area better than he does. He had a head start but he tripped a couple of times. I'm almost on top of him, shove him up against a tree. The knife comes down on his back between the shoulder blades. He lets out one scream and falls. I pull the knife out, wipe it on his arm, clean it, put it back in my sheath. I turn and walk back up towards the cabin. Indians don't respect people's property. If they want it and they have to kill you for it, they will. I was ambushed by two before.

So you feel justified?

I feel justified. I'm not sure whether the tribe will agree.

* * * * * *

Finally, a subject named Dolly made some unsolicited comments about the life of Christ during one regression, and I pursued that line of inquiry in her next regression. The material comes from the point of view of Dolly's Greater Self.

There were several other questions you said you'd research. Do you have answers for them at this time?

What is the question?

I wanted to know about the nature of the Christ figure. Was it in fact the Christ figure who was crucified, or was it a substitute?

He was a man, and he did die on a cross.

Was it the figure of Biblical fame who was crucified?

The same.

So he was the man who walked along the streets carrying the cross?

No, he didn't carry the cross, but he was crucified. There's an awful lot of exaggeration. Others carried the cross.

Was he paraded through the streets for all to see?

He walked. He walked to his death.

There was not a substitute who was crucified? It was the Christ figure who had been preaching?

It was Jesus of Nazareth.

And he was crucified between two thieves?

There were more than three.

He was not recognized by those who crucified him as the Son of God?

He was not.

How was he different from the rest of us?

His faith in himself and his God. The knowledge of self. The belief in the power that he had within himself. Man was a poor figure when he arrived. He was setting an example of what man could be.

He was in fact able to perform many miracles because of this faith in himself and his faith in his God – or are those miracles exaggerated?

Healing power exists. It did then with him, and it still does. His faith healed.

But there is a great deal of legend about his life?

Oh, very much.

If we strip away all the legend and all the misinformation, do we still have a figure who is greater in stature because of his belief in his God and in himself than anyone who has ever lived. Because of strength of belief if nothing else?

Not necessarily greater than anyone else who has ever lived, but greater than most. He's not the only one who believed in himself and in his God. He's an example – a good example.

Did he in fact rise from the dead on Easter morning?

The body remained interred. The Spirit rose.

Why was the body missing from the cave?

He was taken away by those who had him crucified.

What did they do with the body?

Destroyed it.

It has been said by scholars and researchers that Jesus planned his own crucifixion. That the Last Supper was in fact part of the entire plot which culminated in his crucifixion. Did Jesus plan his own death – create the events consciously that led to his crucifixion?

Yes.

In other words, he was not simply the victim of the circumstances of his time?

He created the circumstances of his time.

I see. Was Judas actually a traitor?

[Quickly] No.

Could you explain that?

He was given the silver under false pretences. He was paid when he never thought money was due to him. He wanted to make plans for Christ that Christ would not accept.

What were the plans he wanted to make for Christ?

He wanted him to be known all over – not just in his own little piece of the world.

You're saying that Judas had great insight?

Much. He wanted him to be recognized as a King because he believed he was.

Did all the disciples believe he was the Son of God?

In the end.

Did Jesus want us to believe that his body had arisen from the dead?

No.

So this is part of the legend?

Yes.

What did Jesus actually look like?

He was fair skinned. His hair was light brown – almost a gold – and his beard was darker. He was fairly tall, thin, lean. His eyes were a light shade, not blue, not green, not grey – a combination of all of them.

Your description of him seems to be very different from what his culture or race would seem to suggest.

That's right. Very different.

Did he inherit these traits directly from his mother and father?

As we all do.

So there was a lightness of skin and hair in his parents?

That's right. More in his father.

Was Christ aware from a very young age of his calling? His inner conviction?

Very young.

And he worked with the end of helping people and spreading the word of God?

That was his life.

He put all personal needs aside?

He tried.

Is there anything else you would like to tell me, or elaborate on, relating to the Christ figure?

He was a MAN. A dedicated, trusting, loving man.

You're putting the emphasis on MAN?

Yes.

BEYOND THE SHADOW
OF A DOUBT

≈

*If this counsel or this work be of men, it will come to nought: But
if it be of God, ye cannot overthrow it.*

ACTS 5:38–39

What constitutes proof for one person is mere conjecture for
another. The scientific method demands strict adherence to a
specific protocol that includes controlled experimentation and
repeatable results. Scientific forays into the areas of intuition and
spirituality have generally been frustrating, perhaps because an
emphasis on linearity of thought is unsuitable for probing what
exists beyond space and time. Despite our inability, so far, to apply
science adequately in our quest for understanding of the multi-
dimensional self, a majority of people still *know* that they exist
beyond the physical plane.

Following assertions to irrefutable conclusions is not really necessary for the ordinary person, who is usually willing to accept what
seems reasonable in the light of her or his belief system, experience,
and expectations. Intuitive knowledge is not to be taken lightly,
particularly when it fits into a philosophical framework that
sustains and enhances human life. For most of us, scientific research
provides a validation of what we already know to be correct.

It is not the purpose of this chapter, therefore, to present conclusive evidence from scientific inquiry, but to establish beyond the
shadow of a doubt the validity of 'the most natural of man's convic-
tions'. A large body of material becomes evidential simply because it

is natural – being totally without affectation. The small details of everyday life become the basis for much validation of past-life regressions.

Researching a subject like past lives presents a challenge that is both exciting and frustrating. Some potentially researchable facts lead to greater discoveries, while others become dead-end streets. Leads that go nowhere do not, of course, disprove anything; they simply indicate that the wrong research tools may have been used.

Past lives associated with well-known periods in history or with famous people are neither the most interesting nor the most fruitful to research. There is always the possibility that the subject has knowledge in this lifetime of the events unfolding during regression. To find that an unsophisticated client has pinpointed an obscure Pope in a regression to a medieval lifetime is far more significant evidence for the validity of the experience than would be a recollection of a lifetime wherein the client was a follower of Jesus of Nazareth.

Most of the cases I have researched are those that occurred in the United States or Great Britain during the period from 1750 to the present. Before 1900, records are incomplete and often erroneous, but some reliable ones can be found.

For someone who has never tried to research a minute fact of history, the obstacles are nearly incomprehensible. Who would guess, for example, that trying to verify the wearing of wooden-soled shoes in England in 1900 would involve nearly forty hours of letter writing, library visits, telephone calls, interviews, and more, yet still produce nothing but the general consensus that the information 'does not seem likely to me'. In this particular case, as is fortunately often true, the answer came in a most unexpected way.

The setting was a country dance. An elderly woman sat down next to me and, without any provocation, began chattering about the events of her life. I was wondering what I had done to bring about this verbal onslaught while half-listening to a couple on the other side who were discussing the use of hypnosis in dentistry. My divided attention focused solely on her when she mentioned

England, as I had been engrossed in English past-life research all day.

'My father was furious when I came home that day with mud caked on my wooden shoes', she recalled from the safety of old age. I could not have been more delighted.

'Wooden shoes?' I asked in amazement.

'Oh, yes', she said. 'You know, not really wooden shoes like the Dutch wear, but a wooden sole and leather top. They were store-bought, so I had to be extra careful of them.'

I had to know the year to solve this annoying research puzzle; I hoped it would be as late as 1900. After some mutterings about events and dates and some rather fancy calculations on fingertips, the answer came: 1908. I wanted to hug the old woman, so I danced with her. At that point I knew why I had come to the dance, and I also gained reaffirmation of something I had learned some years earlier. Effort can get in the way of truth; don't expend too much energy in the pursuit of information, but look within and draw the answers to you.

Answers that validate regressions and Greater-Self comments have come in conventional as well as unconventional ways. Another example of trying too hard occurred several years ago when I was attempting to locate a small town in upstate New York near the Canadian border. This was another instance where verification was expected to be an easy matter. I would simply get out some old maps or have researchers check the best maps available ('If it existed it would be on one of these'). I would check the most complete gazetteer available ('This book lists every place down to a population of 35 and it isn't listed'). And presto! No answer.

Then one day I went to a friend's office to pick him up for lunch, and I happened to notice a rather yellowed map on his office wall. It was a map of New York, circa 1835, and there on the Canadian border was the tiny hamlet I had searched for in vain. Armed with this information, I was able to work backwards and find out what had happened to the original name. It turned out that the entire town was obliterated by a reservoir.

The construction of a reservoir over a town is not as uncommon an event as one might think. I ran into it in England as well, and I know from personal experience that it happened in Rhode Island. At the turn of the century the town of Scituate was graced with church spires and a beautiful main street lined with clapboard houses. During the early part of the century, the town fathers decided to flood a large tract of land to provide a dependable water supply for Scituate and nearby communities. That meant that several smaller hamlets would have to disappear forever. Residents were given notice of the impending change, and for hundreds of people it meant taking everything they could carry and moving elsewhere. When the waters came, blacksmith shops, farmland, houses, and barns were inundated, and places like tiny Rockland were no more.

I wondered what kind of information I could get if I pretended that the name of Rockland, Rhode Island came from a regression, so I sought, through the usual research channels, verification of its existence in 1900, several years prior to the reservoir project. From three different library reference departments came these responses:

1. '. . . no such place exists in Rhode Island now and there is no evidence that it ever did.'
2. 'There is at least one Rockland Road in the state but nothing can be found to indicate a place name.'
3. 'Detailed gazetteers do not list a Rockland for the date you mention . . . It all sounds very mysterious to me.'

Anyone in research, of course, is limited by the quality of the tools used, and certainly there are ways, direct and expensive, to find a definitive answer on any issue.

I do past-life research, not to prove that reincarnation is real – for such proof is unnecessary considering the living evidence that abounds in nature – but to help the doubting consciousness relax its role as protector of the ego-self and allow a greater communication with every dimension of the total Self in every time period. There are those who will discount any amount of evidence, no matter how conclusive, if it means that they must change themselves and they do not want to assume that responsibility. In fact, most people who enter counselling for serious life problems want to change their lives but not themselves. Obviously this is unrealistic.

Critics often raise the question of the validity of regression material. Hypnotic references to other customs and traditions are sometimes met with accusations that the material was read or seen in a film or theatrical production. Occasionally someone will charge that the information was researched prior to the session.

I have known a number of my clients quite well personally, and I can attest to the fact that neither deliberate fraud nor childhood memories played a part in their regressions. I know their interests, the influences on them during their formative years, the extent of their education as well as their degree of sophistication, and their sense of honesty. Even without this knowledge, however, it would be virtually impossible to fabricate the intricate personal histories that are so skilfully woven with traditions, customs, dates, places, and – most important – the emotional reactions to people, places, and events.

To my mind, the extraordinary skill required for such realistic 'performances' is more incredible than the assumption that the experience is indeed a genuine past-life memory. How could a simple bricklayer who never graduated from elementary school talk convincingly about life as a Russian ballerina? The man has no interest in theatre or films, has never travelled outside his home state, and had no immigrant grandmother who told stories of the old country.

Sometimes a regression will provide a combination of specifics that seem to be researchable and generalities that are impossible to pinpoint in history. In one regression a young woman, returning to a troubled life in Richmond, Virginia, during the late 1800s, talked about living on Front Street. Most of the regression concerned emotional traumas involving her father, so there was little need for place names or dates.

In the most emotionally charged portion of the story, however, she spoke of returning home late one night in a state of terror because she was several minutes late. Her father, a strict and probably unbalanced disciplinarian, set limits for her every action, though she was already in her thirties. On this occasion, between sobs, she mentioned that walking along Front Street, Highland Park, was 'like walking through the valley of the shadow of death'. Research subsequently proved the existence of a Front Street, east and west from Third Avenue, Highland Park in Richmond. The young woman had never lived outside of San Francisco, had never travelled East, and had no relatives in Virginia. Upon awakening she stated that she must have made up the whole thing. '*Is* Richmond in Virginia?' she asked to my surprise.

One of my most frustrating searches for a place name occurred when I sought to verify the existence of Fordingham, England. Letters to eight postmasters and five librarians in southern England produced negative responses ranging from 'I never have heard of it' to 'No such place exists to my knowledge'. My fourteenth try proved successful; a most welcome letter arrived from the Head Post Office, Portsmouth. Unaware of the magnitude of the event in my mind, the postmaster stated simply: 'I have made enquiries and these reveal that there is a village by the name of Fordingham near Fordingbridge, Hampshire.'

A fascinating account of life in the late nineteenth-century Scotland emerged from a woman who identified herself in a past life as Alex Hendry. Alex was inspired by his mother to overcome his own medical problems and accede to his family's wish that he study medicine at Edinburgh University. In the midst of a vivid description of student life at Edinburgh, Alex mentioned two verifiable facts: that his family home was in Banffshire and that he completed his studies in 1878. There is no conceivable way that my client could have known this information in this lifetime, and yet she spoke with great emotion of struggling with medical studies and of pressures from home. Despite this, a letter to me, dated 19–7–73, from the Keeper of Manuscripts, Edinburgh University, confirms her story: 'Alexander Hendry from Cullen, Banffshire, Scotland, took the degree M. B., C. M. in 1878.'

Quite often the visually oriented client is able to draw pictures of buildings, fashions, and even faces either during or just after the session (with the help of post-hypnotic suggestion). A middle-aged woman who regressed to a life in Sweden felt a vivid awareness of the clothes she and her sisters wore to Christmas Eve service, and after the regression she drew detailed sketches of their outfits. The clothing which she described as 'our holiday best', matched almost perfectly the pictures of young women's finery worn in Sweden in the early 1800s. Afterwards, the woman commented 'I always wondered why I thought "How Great Thou Art" should be sung in a different language. It sounded so beautiful as we sang it in Swedish for the Christmas service.' Research showed that the popular church tune was a Swedish hymn.

Sometimes a subject can write from the personality of a past-life while in a trance, or afterwards through post-hypnotic suggestion. Under the close scrutiny of a graphologist, comparison of the signatures of past and present selves reveal some insights into traits carried over from one life to another.

The two signatures that follow were written by the same subject; sample A was written during a past-life regression, while sample B was written in a fully conscious state. San Francisco handwriting

Sample A

Sample B

expert Marie Sooklaris points out some striking similarities between the two selves, even though the specimens look quite different. (The graphologist was told the samples were from two different people.) After Marie Sooklaris' parallel comments on the subject(s), there is a quotation from the transcript of the regression to the lifetime of Mary. Notice how clearly these excerpts support the graphologist's observations.

Graphologist:

'Exhibits a great deal of intellectual immaturity . . . this writer has a slow mind . . .'

'Has little interest in intellectual pursuits . . . her decision-making process is slow and hesitant.'

From transcript:

I don't do very well in school . . . Father gets angry with me and even offered me a shilling if I brought my studies up a grade . . . and sometimes the girls talk so fast I can hardly tell what they're about.

Graphologist:

'She enjoys . . . social contacts in a protected, familiar environment . . . is self-conscious.'

'She is insecure in unfamiliar surroundings . . .'

From transcript:

I don't mind going to their home . . . I know them all very well. Her mother makes fun of me, but Lucinda doesn't. Oh, yes . . . church is my favourite place. St Mary's always seems friendly to me . . . everyone smiles a lot. It's just a kilometre down the road, you know.

Graphologist:

'. . . acts conventionally out of training.'

'. . . has a need to restrain her behaviour – this would go along with her conventional concepts.'

From transcript:

I wouldn't think of meeting him without proper introductions. It just isn't done, even with those who have little money.

Graphologist:

'She is nervous...' '. . . feels anxious and easily
'... insecure...' confused . . . is inclined to worry
and get nervous . . .'
'Low opinion of self . . . changing
moods.'

From transcript:

'. . . always telling me to stop biting my nails . . . She saw one nail bleeding one day and scolded me severely in front of the whole class.'
'I got sick just thinking of walking in late and had to excuse myself.'

Graphologist:

'Kind and provocative of others . '. . . exhibits kindness and
.. a warm heart ... sensitive.' consideration of others . . . a
sensitive person.'

From transcript:

I always brought her some of the flowers even when she wasn't sick. They seemed to be my responsibility – at least that's the way I looked at it.

The graphologist's comment, in another part of the report, about the physical immaturity of the subject was borne out by the presence of a birth defect that had made one leg considerably shorter than the other. Several other observations from the report were later confirmed by a total of five regressions to the life of Mary:

1. 'This girl has a way of talking herself out of a difficult situation.'
2. 'She is concerned about her needs, which are mainly social and material.'
3. '. . . unconcerned with creatively working solutions to problems.'

4. '. . . heightened sensitivity to environment . . .' (In each of the regressions, Mary mentioned the environment as an important indicator of her moods and attitudes. The flower-strewn countryside was a particularly frequent focal point for her daily life in the small village.)

People do make mistakes during regressions, especially in relating names of people and places and in references to time. Most often the mistakes concerning time are incorrect by units of ten or one hundred. Another problem that sometimes crops up is the combining of the events of several years into a shorter period of time, even to the point of synchronous action; this kind of error can be called fluid time, since one event seems to flow into the next until they all become one.

A good example of this is the regression of Jack to the life as a minister in Connecticut that was disclosed in part in Chapter 9. In one of Jack's sessions, the assassination of Lincoln, the Reconstruction, and the advent of the automobile appeared to have occurred simultaneously. An analysis of the events he cited reveals a fluid time of about thirty-eight years, from 1864 to 1902. Sometimes it is helpful to ask a past self to 'look' at a calendar, but of course many remembrances of past lives predate the common use of the calendar. In a schoolroom scene the subject can be asked what date is written on the papers for the day. People will often reconstruct the date carefully, revealing the process as they do so.

'And what was the date you wrote on your paper in school today?'

'Today? December 11th. Yes, 1911. December 11, 1911.'

Sometimes names of people and places are mispronounced or misspelled in regressions, and occasionally these are corrected by the subject in later sessions. A misspelling can certainly thwart the would-be researcher, since time and place are the keys to establishing validity. Attempts to research a past lifetime in 'Mempstead' in southern England, for example, resulted in an avalanche of negative responses from postmasters and research librarians, until one suggested that perhaps the name was 'Minstead'. Sure enough, many regression specifics proved this to be the case, including the correct names of two local churches and a nearby hamlet.

Though mistakes do occur, accuracy is often absolutely amazing. One client knew nothing consciously of New England, and yet in a regression talked about Boston, naming several out-of-the-way streets and several small neighbouring towns including Duxbury, Rockport, Salem, and Brockton.

The most convincing regressions are not those filled with provable historical data, but those that are seasoned with the subtle flavours of everyday life. My questions are often phrased to test the depth of the regression and the awareness of the period. Queries about modern-day conveniences of which a past self could have no knowledge are met with dismay and puzzlement. The excerpts that follow show some of the subtleties of life that add much realism to events of the past.

*   *   *   *   *   *

What would you like to buy Tim for Christmas?
Oh, a baseball bat, I think.
And how much would you pay for a bat?
Probably a dollar these days.

*   *   *   *   *   *

Does your aunt mind that you collect these insects?
Oh, no, so long as I keep them in the cigar box in the shed. One time
   Lizzy [the dog] got in there and ate my whole collection. She
   knocked the box off the shelf.

*   *   *   *   *   *

How will you get home after shopping?
On the trolley. Father hates to come into the city with the wagon. He
   says people are crazy in the city.

* * * * * *

Have you ever been to California?

No.

Have you ever heard of California?

No, where is that? [The client was born in California and lived there all his life.]

* * * * * *

[Regression set in 1743]

Have you ever heard of America?

No.

That's not familiar to you?

No.

How about the United States?

No.

That doesn't mean anything to you?

No, what is it?

You haven't done much travelling?

Well, just pretty much in the Isles [British Isles] and then I came here to Switzerland.

* * * * * *

What do you do for entertainment. Do you have a TV?

A what?

A TV – a television?

Don't know what that is. For fun we go to a farm, sometimes people come here to ours, and there's always a lot of music, a lot of food, and dancing.

* * * * * *

I bet you enjoy the radio when they leave you alone.
What is a ree-de-o?

* * * * * *

Do you do your sewing on a sewing machine?
I wish there was such a thing – my poor fingers would bless it.

* * * * * *

What do you do for lighting after dark?
Mostly we go to bed, but sometimes I read by the taper.
What is a taper?
You know, wax tapers. I'm sure you've seen them. Where are you
   from, anyway?

* * * * * *

[A regression set in 1895.]
How do you get things you need?
From the store, lots of things we make or grow, and some we get from
   the book.
What do you mean, from the book?
From the catalogue. I was just looking at it this morning. I'd love to
   have the Singer they advertise.
You mean sewing machine?
Yes.
How much would that cost?
I think it said about $12 for the kind I wanted. [Sure enough,
   research produced a catalogue of that year and the prices on the
   Singer ranged from $8.50 to $13.90.]

* * * * * *

Do you ever fly when you go to visit her?

[Laughter] Do you think I'm a bird? People cannot fly.

Don't you think someday man will be able to fly in some machine?

[Laughter] Of course not . . . That's impossible.

So you don't think man will ever go to the moon?

There are some people I would like to send there. [More laughter.]

*   *   *   *   *   *

We planned to meet by the palm.

You said PALM. Did you mean a tree?

A tree, yes, the palm tree just outside town.

And yet you say this is Scotland.

Yes. [I had assumed this was an error of the most obvious kind. Research, however, proved my assumption wrong. The winds and water of the Gulf Stream apparently carry not only warmth but also palm seeds, to the west coast of Scotland. Shakespeare in fact, mentions palms in Scotland.]

*   *   *   *   *   *

What do you do to earn your keep?

I chop wood, work in the garden; I grease the wheels of the wagons, paint the fences, paint the house, and I have to mind the darkies too.

You have to mind the darkies?

Yes.

Who do they work for?

Whoever owns them.

Do you own any?

Oh, no. I may if the old man dies. He may give me his since he has no sons.

*   *   *   *   *   *

You mentioned painting earlier.
Yes.
Do you buy the paint?
Yes. In Atlanta.
What does a can of paint cost?
A large can, about 80.
Is that 80 cents?
Yes. [Date was given as 1860.]

* * * * * *

Tell me what you see.
I see a man in a gold and green silk kimono, small black hat, quite tall, black silk shoes. We are in a marble-like room with black lacquered furniture. There is a garden just outside with a small pool of water. In the room there is a bird in a cage, singing, and flowers everywhere.
Who is this man?
My father. We are going out into the garden now. He has a story for me.
What is the story?
My favourite one about the great wars.
Wars he fought in?
No. They were before his time. He knows of them. He calls them the Ming and Tau Wars, something like that.
Does he talk about anything else you enjoy?
He helps me with my caricatures by telling me stories about each one. And he tells me about the animals in the sky. He has a story for each one of them too.
You mean the star formations?
Yes, the outlines of animals. He shows me where they are in the sky.
You said you were going on a picnic?
Yes, for a holiday.
What did you take with you?
Just some food . . . black bread, sausage, cider, you know . . . just what

we could carry in the hamper.

In the what?

In the hamper.

What is a hamper?

[Irritated] A hamper . . . a basket for food . . .

* * * * * *

Where did you and Joseph first meet?

The first time?

Yes.

In the scullery.

What is the scullery?

It's where we take care of all the dirty things . . . dishes . . . a footman also helps take things in and out to the dining area. We met in the scullery.

* * * * * *

Where do you live?

Montmartre.

Do you go to church?

Yes.

What is the name of it?

Sacred Heart.

[This client had never been in France and was not a student of French history.]

* * * * * *

What do your brothers want to do?

One wants to go to the sea . . . maybe he'll talk the other one into going to sea . . . [Puzzled] I don't know what sea is . . . they talk about boats . . . one drew a picture of a boat . . . George drew a picture of it . . . it was funny.

You've never seen a boat?
Just the picture that George drew.
[The client lives near the water and is very familiar with boats of all
    kinds in this life.]

* * * * * *

Comparisons of word choices between regressive and conscious
answers are sometimes interesting.
Regression response: How do you spell Jeanette?
It's J E A N E double T E.
Conscious response: How do you spell Jeanette?
J E A N E T T E.

* * * * * *

Regression: How far away is it?
Just a stone's throw down the road.
*Conscious: How would you say something is not very far away down the
    road?*
Down the road a piece.

* * * * * *

Regression: What is the year?
1890.
And who is the ruler?
Victoria, of course.
Conscious: Who was the English ruler in 1890?
Edward something, I think.

* * * * * *

Where do you live?
The United Kingdom.

Conscious: What would you call England, Scotland, Wales, and Northern Ireland?

Great Britain.

* * * * * *

What coinage do you use?

Pennies, shillings, crowns, half-crowns, and paper pounds.

You use crowns?

Yes.

And what year is this?

1874.

[The crown was discontinued in 1934.]

* * * * * *

Regression: How much do you weigh?

About nine and a half stones, I should imagine. [Equivalent of 133 lb.]

How many pounds is that?

[Chuckle] How does money come into it?

I meant pounds as weight.

Never heard of such a thing.

* * * * * *

The most convincing evidence for the validity of past-life regressions is the very ordinary way in which people express themselves. These remembrances are characterized by the entire gamut of human reactions – the laughter, the tears, the scepticism, the conviction, the fear, the courage, the hatred and the love. All of this comes forth from the subject in a casual and unselfconscious way. The material may be intensely dramatic, but it is never dramatized.

The precision with which the Mind calls forth that material strictly relevant to the purpose of the person in regression is truly

remarkable. It is a process at once so complex and so brilliantly efficacious that to observe it is to be convinced beyond the shadow of a
doubt.

13

AS YE SOW

≈

Whatsoever a man soweth, that shall he also reap.

GALATIANS 6:7

It matters not how strait the gate,
How charged with punishments the scroll,
I am the master of my fate:
I am the captain of my soul.

WILLIAM ERNEST HENLEY, *INVICTUS*

With few exceptions, people who seek past-life counselling misunderstand the concept of karma. Invariably those who have had some exposure to Eastern philosophies or to metaphysics think of karma as a mystical force of retribution that makes one pay for past misdeeds. Thus those who are unhappy feel that their misery is a result of 'bad karma', that in a past life they inflicted grave harm on others, so that now they are paying off their 'karmic debt'. I have heard many intelligent individuals say that they will need two or three more lives to pay off their karmic debt. This reveals a fundamental misunderstanding about karma.

If we begin by identifying God as Primal Cause and the Universe as Evolving Effect, we can then define karma as the universal principle that expresses that relationship. Karma is the universal principle out of which ALL evolves; it is the cause and effect of the universe. Karma is the general tendency or direction of all things. It is the dynamic tension between event and result. (In human beings stress, both mental and physical, represents this tension unresolved.)

Within this most pervasive of all energies there is free choice and creative expression of everything in nature. The Eastern world calls this creative choice *dharma*. We either use it or ignore it, but it is always there as part of the karmic energy.

Everything in nature is comprised of events that lead to and result in other events. We could say that we live in an ocean of karmic energy. There is no escape from it, nor is there any need to escape from it. We are not trapped like insects in a bottle, judged by outside agencies and suffering the sentences of past misdeeds. Karma is personal and internal because of our complete interrelatedness with the universe.

If we wish to view karma in terms of debts, then we must see that they are debts that we owe to ourselves and that we pay off at the appropriate time and place in a manner we find to be fitting. As creative beings, we have the innate ability to erase every debt and reach a state of spiritual solvency, a perfect balance where we are no longer focused on compensation for earlier actions. It is easy to see why karma is sometimes called the law of compensation.

Ted, a thirty-four-year old insurance salesman, recently expressed the common misunderstanding of karma when he stated flatly to me that 'my life is falling apart because of my bad karma. I must have done something terrible in the past – like murder someone – and now I am getting my just desserts.'

He proceeded to narrate a sorry saga of divorce, business failures, and illnesses. He said nothing of the positive aspects of his life, such as his natural ability to play almost any musical instrument at the first try, his ease in learning complex mathematical concepts, or his grace and agility in sports. Like so many others, Ted assumed that only the limitations and failures of life were karmic, and the good things were only natural and outside the realm of karma. To understand karma and to discover the causes of his misery, Ted chose a series of regressions, each one intended to uncover some piece of the past that would explain the present.

In the first regression, Ted found himself in ancient Mexico and in a relationship with the person who in the present lifetime is his former wife. Ted was then a master teacher and highly respected leader who had learned the art from his father. However, he had no children of his own to whom he could pass the traditions, so he had taken on a young male protégé (the wife) who seemed to be sincere in his efforts to learn the closely guarded tribal healing secrets, which combined ceremonies with complex formulations of herbs and roots.

The apprentice grew impatient for Ted to die and leave him in a position of prestige and power, so he killed the teacher and made the crime look like a case of accidental poisoning.

This same person, Ted's wife in this lifetime, again betrayed him through unfaithfulness and finally abandoned him for one of her many lovers. At the end of this session Ted commented with some surprise 'I was a victim, not a murderer!' Little did he realize that the had played the role of victim repeatedly through the centuries, as subsequent regressions would reveal.

In the second regression Ted found himself panning for gold during the great Gold Rush. Betrayal was again the result of Ted's blind trust in another person. This time it was a man who gave all the appearance of reliability and honesty, but at the end jumped the claim they had both worked hard to prospect, leaving Ted with little more than the clothes on his back.

The third regression found Ted an accomplished musician in the eighteenth-century French court. His music was his life – so much so that, as the structure of his life began to crumble around him, he placed more and more attention on his music. As events came to a climax, he was falsely accused of conspiracy and beheaded.

In regression after regression, Ted uncovered the same theme in a variety of forms: he was too trusting of people he did not really know. As a result of this information, Ted became aware that insight is more valuable and essential in understanding people and their motives than is outer sight. He had chosen a number of lives for himself just to realize this. He was now able to see the effects of causative events and his eyes were opened to the reality of situations occurring in the present. Ted came to understand that the unhappy, frustrating conditions of the present can and do extend far back into the past, but are not necessarily the direct opposites of present conditions. The truism that appearances are deceiving finally had clarity for him. Ted realized also that karma is the flow of energy between *all events* and their outcomes, rather than just the negative ones.

Josh, the alcoholic of Chapter 1, is a good example of the manifestation of effect in this lifetime (his destructive drinking) which derives from the causative event (the drunken killing of his pregnant squaw) of a past life. Until Josh got in touch with that event, his prospect for health and happiness was totally blocked.

For the many people, Josh included, who seek escape routes and reject personal responsibility, 'bad karma' has become a seemingly legitimate way to absolve themselves of direct and positive action that could create happiness. Such an avoidance of appropriate action, of course, strengthens one's image as victim and results in psychological suicide.

Understanding karma helps us to see ourselves as part and parcel of the universe. If we know that we are creative beings of potential, and that we ourselves engineer all outcomes (that is, the events of our lives), then we can begin to assume full control of the creative process and steer ourselves towards fulfilment and happiness.

People just do not know that they can assume responsibility for their lives. It has never occurred to them that their suffering is the result of an unwillingness to confront the events of the past. Knowing that another way exists is a discovery that opens doors for people and is a remarkably freeing experience.

In nature we see karma constantly in operation, from the circling of electrons around the nucleus of the atom to the orbiting of planets around the suns of the universe. In physics we learn that for every action there is an equal and opposite reaction. A pendulum pulled one way will move back beyond the centre to the opposite side. A stone cast in the still lake will send its ripples to the distant shore. Everywhere in nature – in every facet of nature – we find cause and effect that is immediate and appropriate. Karma does not wait.

Effect follows cause as surely and as quickly as the thunder follows the lightning. Sometimes our perception of the result lags behind the occurrence itself, but cause establishes the energy for effect whether or not it is recognized.

Buddha explained karma beautifully and simply in the statement '... effect follows cause as the wheel of the cart follows the foot of the ox'. Jesus set forth this most universal of all principles in a similar way when he said 'As ye sow, so also shall we reap.' And we learn from the Bible that he who lives by the sword shall die by the sword. A single lifetime would surely not allow a person time to resolve all the conditions established or to reap all the benefits of a life of self-lessness. In Mark 10:28–31, for example, there is a listing of rewards that could hardly be bestowed in one lifetime.

Would an all-loving God limit His most highly evolved creation to one opportunity to discover the nature of his being, work out all his lessons, and grow to perfection? That would be analogous to expecting a child to attend one day of classes and then enter the mainstream of professional life as a physicist, a psychologist, or a physician. Such a comparison may seem absurd to some, but to those who understand causes and effect, having only one lifetime to work out hate, jealousy, possessiveness, and greed and to achieve unconditional love – to believe completely in the manifestation of spiritual power, to develop potentials fully, to perceive Divine Order in the universe and to work with it – is even more absurd.

Even a cursory consideration of karma makes it readily apparent that karma is perfect justice, for it is totally objective, totally without emotion or politics or plea bargaining. No one has the edge over anyone else because of money, power, or position. The effect is always in direct proportion to the cause, both negatively and posi-tively. Karma gives meaning to turning the other cheek. When we understand karma it can easily be seen that it is not weakness to fail to react to threats. There is strength in the knowledge that the universe is at work at all times, always setting the record straight.

Many religions have viewed karma as a system of reward and punishment that awaits all of us at death. This simplistic view fails to recognize that karmic forces are constant and consistent, so that many 'debts' are 'paid off' immediately after they are created. The Day of Judgement is every day, every hour, every minute that we live – both in and out of physical reality.

Karma is not a fatalistic doctrine, for it does not recognize Fate as a force in the universe, any more than it recognizes evil as a natural thing. We are not tainted by Adam's sin, but by our own. Each of us is the creator of our own character, and if we create with full conscious awareness of all our yesterdays, our tomorrows will be much more than attempts to absolve ourselves of the 'sins' of the past. Karma and Fate could not possibly be considered synonymous, for Fate presupposes a sort of captivity while karma provides freedom as we create the conditions for it. Only when we fail to exercise this creative responsibility does life become a prison.

Karmic responsibility begins with our thoughts. Through thoughts we create expectations and the fulfilment or disappointments of those expectations creates emotions. It is the emotional essence that triggers events and sends energy waves out from us into the universe, where they affect everything just as the pebble thrown into the lake. It is the emotional essence that is forever registered in us and carried from lifetime to lifetime.

Henry Ford commented on this concept when he said:

> We all retain, however faintly, memories of past lives. We frequently feel that we have witnessed a scene or lived through a moment in some previous existence. But that is not essential; it is the essence, the gist, the result of experience, that are valuable and remain with us.

(QUOTED IN *THE ESOTERIC TRADITION*, II, 641, BY G. DE PURUCKER)

Thus we see the best evidence of karma in action with our everyday thoughts. We think negatively and everything seems to go wrong; we think positively and things seem to fall into place. The Apostle Paul may have stated this best when he pointed out that 'As a man thinketh, so is he'. And Jesus affirmed this same concept with 'It is done unto you as you believe'. We are at all times where we are because of the thoughts we have allowed ourselves to entertain in the past, whether that past be a second ago or fifty lifetimes ago.

Thoughts and their resulting emotions build character. This is a predictable process where chance has no place. It is a product of the law of karma, which cannot err.

Someone once said that thought is the seed of destiny. If we think of the mind as a garden that may be well-cared for or allowed to become overrun with weeds, we can see that whether fertile ground is cultivated or not, it will produce life. If the seeds of destiny are care-fully chosen and planted, a rich and full harvest will result. If they are carelessly chosen, or none are consciously planted, weeds will surely grow. Each of us has the responsibility to be vigilant for weeds of thought that can create a jungle of confusion in which we will become lost.

Because we wish to live well, we cannot afford to let the garden be overrun through lack of concern. Complacency produces perplexity at the very least, and total confusion at the worst. A garden of weeds produces no food and we literally starve ourselves physically, mentally, emotionally and spiritually. This, our most basic responsi-bility, is summed up skilfully in the following words: 'Sow a thought and reap an act, sow an act and reap a habit, sow a habit and reap a character, sow a character and reap a destiny.'

Some modern scientists recognize the importance of thoughts as causative agents with karmic effects. William Tiller of Stanford Research Institute, has said 'by our thoughts and actions today, we tangibly create the events we meet in our future tomorrows.' (This quotation is from the January 1974 issue of *Science of Mind* magazine).

Sometimes it appears that someone is operating outside the law of karma – that things are either better or worse for that person than they should be. We must never forget that appearances are deceiving; our eyes and ears provide us with much information, but it is never objectively received, since our expectations always colour our sensory impressions. We hear what we want to hear, see what we want to see.

It is easy to view the poor and the powerless as victims of some cruel fate, and the rich and famous as inheritors of a great deal of luck. Such is not the case. The wealthy person may, in fact, be miserable because of fame and fortune, and the wealth may be a difficult karmic experience that has been established for a growth opportunity. The money becomes the challenge, not the salvation. If the rich and famous person fails to love himself and others more fully because the money stands in the way, then the lesson has not been learned.

Even those who seem to get off 'scot free' are not truly free, since conscience works at some level in everyone, even those who kill in cold blood and seem to have no remorse. Effect does follow cause at the deepest levels of existence.

Low self-esteem and fear bring about the murder of the self – the slow, erosive kind of killing that takes place insidiously over a long period of time. In cosmic terms this self-assassination is just as serious a mistake as the physical murder would be. When we feel negative about ourselves, the feelings generate more and more negativity about everything and everyone, and we create a self-perpetuating destiny of doom.

Recalling past lives helps us to realize that we do not have to cower in the corner of life, quivering with emotions and negative thoughts. We can and must take hold of the present, confront the past, and set ourselves free.

A simple, three-step process dissolves karmic debt faster than any other action:

1. Recognize the past by confronting it.
2. Feel purposeful and powerful.
3. Love as unconditionally as possible.

For those who hate more than they love, the last step is the most difficult. Such people must grow by stages. First comes understanding, then acceptance, then liking, loving, and releasing.

Past-life regression allows us to confront original thoughts and the resulting emotional traumas and to disarm them – for they are often like time bombs that we have carried for centuries. Then, breathing freer, without fear and confusion, we can act in such a way that new karma is established which will produce positive, self-imposed rewards.

Acting to resolve old negativities and sending out unconditional love will reap a harvest of spiritual growth, contentment, and abundance beyond anything experienced before. That is the glory and the promise implicit in the universal law of karma.

CROSSING OVER

≈

They will come back, come back again,
As long as the red Earth rolls.
He never wasted a leaf or a tree
Do you think He would squander souls?

RUDYARD KIPLING

The old man sat huddled in the corner of the room. I could hardly see him in the dim light afforded by three candles, but I could hear him softly crooning to himself as he rocked back and forth. 'Sunrise, sunset, swiftly go the year . . .'

'He's been like this for months', the old man's daughter said, 'focused on death.' The room was in stark contrast to the rest of the nursing home, which was brightly lit and filled with activity. Her father paid no attention to us as we stood before him, but when I introduced myself he seemed to pull himself into the present for a moment, looking at me with mournful eyes.

'I am going to die', he said matter-of-factly. But then a tear trickled down one cheek. 'I am so afraid.'

'All of us will die, and many are afraid', I told him, ' but there is no need to fear. Let me tell you what I have learned about the death experience.'

For two months the old man and I met weekly, and by the end of that time he had resolved some of his fear and rejoined the world of the nursing home, determined to enjoy the days remaining to him.

It is safe to say that nothing evokes more fear and dread in human beings than the prospect of death. No single word raises more persistent and complex questions about the nature of humankind. From time immemorial people have feared death, ignored it, rejected it, been confused by it, and done what little they could to delay it. They have attempted to deal with it through myths, religions, and schools of philosophy. In fact, there are those who feel that philosophy is nothing more than the study of the problems related to death. Schopenhauer, for instance, called death 'The truly inspiring genius of philosophy'. Death has been a ubiquitous inspiration for music, art, and literature. Perhaps Michaelangelo put this best when he stated 'No thought exists in me which death has not carved with a chisel.'

The subject of death is hedged in with paradoxes and ambiguities. On the one hand, we do everything possible technologically to prolong life – or the appearance of life. On the other hand, we go to absurd lengths to avoid the subject entirely, for death conjures up the same feelings of embarrassment and discomfort as did abortion or venereal disease a few decades ago.

Even worse, we tend to view death as the embodiment of all that is ugly and evil in humankind, as though some angry god were punishing us for our transgressions. From earliest times we have believed that the body of a dead person is dirty and untouchable. Children are rushed off to relatives to be spared the horror of having to confront death. We use euphemisms like 'pass away' to avoid saying the word *death*. We try to make the dead look as though they are merely sleeping. We withhold the truth of terminal illness from patients. All of these tactics, and many others, are attempts to avoid confrontation with our own feelings of inadequacy in dealing with death. Facing death means facing the ultimate question of the meaning of life.

Death on a large scale is always easier to deal with, for it is less personal and more removed from our reality of self. According to Thomas Lewis in *Lives of a Cell*,

We can sit around the dinner table and discuss war involving sixty million volatilized human deaths, as though we were talking about

bad weather; we can watch . . . bloody death every day, in colour, on films and television, without blinking back a tear. It is when the numbers of dead are very small and very close, that we begin to think in scurrying circles. At the very centre of the problem is the naked cold deadness of one's self, and the only reality in nature of which we can have absolute certainty, and it is unmentionable, unthinkable.

In refusing to acknowledge death as a personal event that we will experience, we do everything we can to ensure our hold on life, even as life wanes in us. In short, we desperately, even obsessively, want to go on. We want this despite our awareness that long lives are not necessarily happy lives – particularly in a society oriented to youth and beauty that has little patience with old age, weakness, and dependency.

People who have experienced clinical death (that is, who have 'died' for a few minutes and been revived) relate interesting stories of separation from the physical body and the ability to look at it and at surrounding events from the 'outside'. Some tell of their reluctance to return to the body once it is coerced into working condition once again.

For those who have had such close encounters with death, the experience has in most cases removed all fear. Those who have not had such a moment of truth generally find their attitude towards death to be whatever the culture prescribes it to be, for the reaction to death – perhaps more than any other concept – is a product of the culture of which we are a part. Only a confrontation with our eternalness can dispel cultural prescriptions. People are beginning to be willing to examine their feelings about death; possible 50 per cent of those who come to the Alternative Therapies Council do so because of fear – and curiosity – about death.

To understand the meaning of death, we must look at life. This is not because death is the opposite of life, as is commonly supposed, but because death is an extension of life marked by a cessation of physical functioning.

Historically we have made the erroneous assumption that where there is no obvious motion there is no life. Let us consider life as process in motion. All things of nature are alive, for everything is a process, or system of processes, in motion. There is movement in all things even when the eye cannot detect it. The word *life* could be an acronym for Limitless Integration of Fields of Energy. Thus even when death occurs there is still life, for energies continue to exist and one of these energies carries memory and consciousness. (Recall the experiments with the L-fields in Chapter 3.)

We have always tested reality by what our senses tell us. The cessation of heartbeat and brain function have therefore led us to believe that the end has come, the final curtain has been drawn. If we are to believe those who have experienced clinical death and those who have recounted past-life experiences of death in hypnosis, such is not the case. Even the 'dead' physical body is alive with activity, for electrons continue to circle their nuclei in tremendously complex continuing processes.

Common sense tells us that death as we ordinarily perceive it cannot be part of life. Yet changes of form and substances occur as part of the life we know. The shedding of the physical form is one of those changes that is not all that different from birth or puberty. All are part of a process that is predictable – a letting go of the old and a new way of dealing with the most immediately perceived reality. Certainly we do not mourn when a child is born, and yet regressions to birth reveal it as a time of great suffering, great trauma, and incredibly rapid change of form. A newborn seems to change right before our eyes. Puberty involves a dropping away of the child's body and a taking on of the adult form. It is, in a way, the death of the child and the birth of the adult, and yet no one mourns.

Birth and death are nothing more and nothing less than the entering and leaving of physical reality. When we view our lives – all our births and deaths – from a higher perspective, we sense a flashing into and out of the physical plane as in an instant, each lifetime like the lighting and extinguishing of a candle. The Hindu sees death this way: death is the candle burning low that, just before extinguishing, lights a new candle, and so on to infinity. For Hindus and Buddhists, another lifetime is stark reality, and to never take on human form again, a romantic fantasy. Ralph Waldo Emerson had this to say:

> *All things subsist and do not die, but only retire a little from sight and afterwards return again. Nothing is dead: Men feign death and endure mock funerals and mournful obituaries, and then they stand looking out the window, sound and well, in some new strange disguise.*

For most religions, birth is the beacon of death. In general, religions seem to exist because they offer a complicated system of preparation for death, and yet this preparation is unnecessarily filled with darkness and foreboding. No matter what the religious orientation of those who come from past-life regressions, their reports of earlier death experiences are remarkably consistent. Death is a time of transition, a time of peace, beauty and freedom, a time of letting go of the old and wornout, a time of moving into the ever-new and yet familiar.

Perhaps the most complimentary epitaph we can ever ascribe to anyone is that they have spent their body wisely, for to spend means to use and profit by. If we profit by our physical forms we can release them with little reluctance. To do this requires placing great emphasis on the here and now, on living life to the fullest, on taking risks and exploring new horizons: there is no saving of the self for some later time.

It is important to realize that all transitions from one place to another or from one form to another take time. Changing jobs, moving to a new home, adding or subtracting pounds – all take time. The same is true of birth and death! The choice of parents was not a rash decision. The decision to die is not a hasty decision either, even when sudden death occurs through heart attack, car accident, or war. It is a process that is many years, or even lifetimes, in the making. People are dying all the time, all around us, for death is a mental state long before it is a physical one. Even the person who appears healthy and fully alive may, in fact, be in the process of preparing for transition, for crossing over into a different realm.

We can look at death as the process by which humanity grows and evolves. New consciousness with new bodies means new ideas and new progress. Death and rebirth might be compared to falling asleep and then awakening refreshed and revitalized, ready and eager to begin working in new directions with new inspirations. The old and wornout dies to make way for the new, for little progress can be made with tired bodies and tired minds.

The death transition can be compared to the change that occurs when a caterpillar turns into a butterfly. The butterfly's world is totally different from what it used to be, and it seems likely that it remembers nothing of being a furry, crawling creature. Emerging from the cocoon, it is light and filled with new energies as it ascends to the sky.

For humans, feelings of lightness, floating, and freedom are the hallmarks of death. Time after time people report these sensations during regressions to former deaths, and the reports are so similar that one is bound to assume they are all accurately recalling what happens.

In terms of energy changes, the physical vibration gradually slows down and transfers over to the etheric vibration (the energy that surrounds and infuses the physical body). There is a dropping away of the personality, that individual mask that each of us wears for others to see. The feeling of lightness increases as the physical body is shed. A change of focus gradually occurs, so that the dying person can view life from within and from without the physical eyes. Eventually there is total separation, all awareness having transferred to the non-physical energy self, which is then able to look down upon the vacated physical form.

Certain statements can be made about the death transition because they have been reported time and time again by persons in hypnotic regressions.

1. Where there was deformity before, or mutilation during, death, there is wholeness afterwards. A missing arm, for instance, is

seen and felt as though it were never missing.

2. Despite emotions and feelings just before death, a uniform tranquillity and deep contentment infuses consciousness after the transition.
3. Incredibly accurate and detailed perception is part of the after-death state.
4. A tragic and sudden death means a faster return to the earth plane, sometimes only hours or days later.
5. The longest lives seem to produce the longest absences from the earth plane (i.e., the longest time between incarnations).

Some people report being met by loved ones. For some, guides and teachers are present, and for others, a white or blue-white light of the Christ figure is present and directing the way. Invariably there is a desire to release everything of the lifetime just concluded.

Suicide is followed by a state of temporary confusion and intense regret, followed by an understanding and awareness of the crime committed against self through over-identification with physical reality. The tendency is to reincarnate quickly in order to face once more that which seemed too overwhelming.

The following word-for-word tape transcriptions reveal the consistency of the death experience despite the varying backgrounds and religious affiliations of the persons speaking. Notice the repeated words and phrases throughout the examples.

* * * * * *

The subject was a Roman Catholic man, age fifty-two:

Where are you?

I'm in bed. I can breathe only a little. My lungs are full of fluid. The fever is high.

Do you know that you are dying?

Yes. I can feel myself letting go of life. It is too much effort to hold on

. . . and too painful.

Go ahead and tell me what happens.

I died.

How did it feel?

I just stopped breathing and left my body. I suddenly felt very light, very light and free, no more pain. I could breathe now . . . not really breathe, of course, but the feeling was that I could breathe. I had almost forgotten what breathing easy was like. The whole room seemed light . . . a soft glowing light, but I don't know where it was coming from.

Where did you go?

I stayed above my body watching. The landlady came back into the room with a bowl of soup for me. She didn't know I had died, that I was so close to dying when she left me to get the soup.

What did she do?

She gasped as she came close to the bed. She said my name and then screamed 'Sacre bleu', dropping the tray with the soup. Then she ran from the room, screaming. I felt sorry for her, that I was causing her so much trouble, but I smiled to myself, too, because it was so funny that she thought I was dead.

What happened then?

She brought the doctor a short time later, but she stayed outside the room, wringing her hands in her apron while the doctor poked at my body. He then drew the covers over my face and told Mrs Jamiel to make arrangements for my burial. She cried as she walked away from the room.

Were you aware of your burial?

Oh, yes. I was buried in a pauper's grave with a cement marker.

Did you stay around the place where you had died?

No, I had other places to go. I wasn't interested any more in that place.

* * * * * *

The next subject was a thirty-five-year-old man, Fundamentalist Church, father a minister:

Go right up to the time of your death. I want you to tell me how you died.

A baby . . .

Tell me about it.

It hurt . . .

And what happened?

I died.

Did you realize you were dying?

No, not at first.

What was it like when you realized it?

Separation.

How did you know you had died?

Because I could see me.

You could see your body?

Yes.

Where were you, that you could see your body?

In the room, just above.

Was anyone there with you when you died?

Yes, the doctor was there.

Did he say anything when you died?

Yes, he said 'Hortense is gone'.

Did the baby live?

It was alright then.

So you died giving birth?

Yes.

What happened after you died?

I was buried.

Could you see your burial?

I knew of it, but I wasn't right there. I had no interest in it.

At the moment of death and separation, what did you do?

I just sort of drifted around in the room for a while.

And then?

And then they took the rest of me away and I didn't know quite what to do so I waited.

What were you waiting for?

Direction.

And you got it?

Yes. Something . . . Someone told me I didn't need to stay around there any longer. Something came and was with me giving me great comfort.

What was that something?

At first I thought it was an angel, but then I realized I shouldn't call it that.

What should you have called it?

A portion of me . . . the spirit form.

So death of the physical body was not very difficult for you?

No. I just slipped out. It didn't hurt. I wasn't even concerned about
the baby at that point.

*　*　*　*　*　*

Woman, age twenty-nine, a (northern) Baptist with no belief in
reincarnation and acceptance of the concepts of heaven and hell:

How old were you when you died?

Forty-four.

And what was it that caused your death?

They said influenza. They said so many people died of it. It was all
over the world.

What year did you die?

Nineteen eighteen. I think it was October, October 20.

Was anyone with you when you died?

No.

What was it like after you died?

I could see my body.

How could you see yourself?

I had a blue dress on . . . blue, silky . . . a dress somebody had bought
me to be buried in.

Did you know you were going to die?

Yes. I was so sick. I knew I couldn't get better. After I died, people were coming and talking about why everyone was dying. Many, many people died.

Can you tell me about your funeral?

They had us all in rows, and I was down one part of it. The first stone to the right. Oh, there were a lot of others all lined up.

Where did they bury you, Mary?

In a big field near a hill just outside the village. They put up a small cement stone with no name or anything on it. All the others had markers too. So many people died they had to dig a special place for us. There wasn't any room in the graveyard.

Were you able to see the village after you died?

I came back to see.

What did you want to see?

Just wanted to look at it, to see what it looked like, but I didn't stay.

* * * * * *

A woman, age forty-four, religious upbringing mixed – from Catholic to Episcopalian to metaphysical:

Go ahead to the time of your death.

The boat went over. A great big wave hit it and it went over. I am going around and around. I don't know how to swim.

What happens at the moment of your death?

I'm over the trees.

So you left your physical body?

Yes.

Was there any pain?

No. I was there in my body and then I wasn't. I didn't mind leaving at all. It felt good.

* * * * * *

A woman, age forty-six, agnostic:

Tell me what happened at the time of your death.

There was light. I was light, too. Someone was sitting by me – my grandmother Mary – by the bed in spirit form. I was so tired. I knew I was dying. I was old and tired.

What is it like to die?

It is like a weight being lifted. You feel much lighter. It is intense lightness and brightness. There is no fear any more.

You were aware of what was happening around you?

Yes. I could look down on my physical body. It's so ugly, I don't need it anymore. I'm glad to go.

* * * * * *

A woman, age fifty, mixed religious upbringing, sceptical of life after death, fear of death quite real:

Let's go to the time of your death.

I know I'm dying, and I'm ready. I'm sixty-six years old. That is quite old for my family. I have white hair. I'm ready.

Are you afraid?

No, I have no fear. I've had a good life.

What is the cause of your death?

Old age. The body is worn out . . . parts letting go. Herman is still alive and is sad to see me go. He is here crying and my children are not here.

Tell me about the moment of death.

I let go and I drift upward. I can see my body. I am above it, looking down. It was very early in the morning. Herman knew I had died.

What happened then?

I stayed around for a while just looking, and then I drifted up and there was someone to meet me – like my guardian angel – spirits from the other side to show me the way. They spoke without words, gave me much comfort. I was glad to go to the other side. It's so peaceful and beautiful. Very light, clear blues. It's almost like another world, similar in so many ways to the earth and yet so different. I was a spirit with a different kind of body form . . . a form, an energy form each one of us had . . . so we had our own identities . . . not diffused . . . coming from one source with its own identity. I could have seen earth if I chose to, but I chose to let it go. I chose to no longer keep track of my husband or children.

* * * * * *

A woman, age forty-two, liberal religious upbringing:

Go up to the time of your death. Where are you when you die?

Near the Arno River. I was walking near the river and I was attacked by robbers.

How old were you?

Forty-six.

What was it like for you when you were attacked?

I didn't believe it.

Did you linger for a while or did you die immediately?

I died. They stabbed me in the back.

What was the death experience like for you?

I was surprised. I thought I was still alive.

Was there any pain?

Not really. Only for an instant.

Could you see your body after you died?

I was crumpled in a heap, face down.

How could you see your body if you were dead?

I was looking down on it. I was about twelve feet above it.

Were you a spirit?

I was me, looking at it.

And then what happened?

Then I went back to my house, to where my wife was.

Was she aware that you were dead?

No. I could see her working in the kitchen.

Could she see you?

No.

Did you try to make yourself known?

I didn't think that I could. I don't think I tried.

*How did you feel, knowing that your dead body was out there by the river
and your wife did not know?*

I wanted to protect her.

Did you stay with her from then on as a spirit?

I stayed with her until . . . until she was all right again.

After she had recovered from your death?

Yes.

And then where did you go?

I went to another place.

What was it like?

It was green and sunny. I seem to be just at the edge of the place, not in it.

Did you have a feeling of contentment, or do you feel sorrowful that you had to cross over?

I feel both. The beauty of the place and the sorrow for my wife.

* * * * * *

A young man, eighteen, liberal Christian upbringing:

Describe your death.

I was driving along in my new car, going sort of fast, trying to break it in. All of a sudden this car pulls out of an intersection right in front of me. I push on the brakes and skid . . .

What happened then?

I hit the side of the car . . . my chest hurts . . . the steering wheel is pushed up against it. Neck is broken, it hurts . . . my stomach hurts a whole lot.

Go ahead to the moment of your death.

I was released, the pain stopped, eased away . . . relief.

Where were you when you died?

In the ambulance.

Yeah. It was . . . I was sorta standing inside the ambulance, looking down.

Was anybody saying anything?

Not really. The attendant seemed . . . bothered.

How long did you watch your body?

Not very long. Didn't seem to be any reason to.

Where did you go when you left your body?

It was dark, quiet . . . resting.

What happened after you finished resting?

I started thinking about my death and what I would be as an actor.

So you carried the desire to be an actor with you?

Yeah. I guess I wanted to be . . . to do . . . more than what I had done.

Is this why you came back to human form again so quickly?

Yeah. It's what I really wanted to do.

*   *   *   *   *   *

A woman, thirty-four, various religious affiliations, most recently Unity:

Let's go ahead in time.

I don't want to go ahead in time.

Why is that?

I become very lonely.

What do you do about your loneliness?

I try to see my friends, but they have no time.

Go to the moment of your death. How did you die?

I killed myself.

How did you do that?

I jumped from a building.

Had you planned it for a long time?

No. I didn't plan it.

What made you do it?

Desperation.

What was it like after you died?

I was still lost for a while. It was like going through a whirlwind, looking for light. I have much regret about taking my life.

What ended your confusion?

I saw my parents.

They had died before you?

Yes.

How did that solve your confusion?

I had a feeling of understanding . . . a realization of what happened, of what I had stupidly done. I came to understand myself in spirit for the journey. A plan had failed.

By 'plan' do you mean that lifetime?

Yes.

[And then, from a perspective of great altitude and wisdom, the answers continued.]

Is the after death state the same for all those who take their own lives?

Yes, in a way it is. They are not supposed to do it. They don't know what they are doing.

A person should never take his or her own life?

You cannot say 'never'. There are circumstances, like severe illness . . . but suicide is done with a feeling of turmoil, resentment, and uncertainty, so for most people it accomplishes nothing.

Is there suffering in the next lifetime as a result of this action?

It depends on the individual soul. There is no general rule.

Is it different for everyone, then?

We each have a decision to make. Once they realize where they are, the decision will likely be incarnation again under circumstances best designed to learn the lesson not learned in the lifetime that ended prematurely. It solves nothing, nothing.

* * * * * *

A woman, twenty-four, Protestant:

I'm lying in some straw, choking from the smoke. The flames are all around me . . . I can't breathe, I can't move. I'm going fast. Now suddenly I'm light. I'm floating, light, expanding . . . I have a new body, I'm rid of the old. I am free, rising to the light. It is just there above me and I'm rising into it and it comforts me . . . such a peace and beauty and warmth. It is so loving I am unafraid.

* * * * * *

A man, twenty-one, Fundamentalist:

Tell me about the very moment of death.

A feeling of . . . not quite certain . . . somehow never leaving and . . . get up and open the door and see the other people . . . I'm very much afraid.

Let's go to a moment or two after your death.

[Sigh] Oh, what a relief! I see a cabinet standing over against the wall.

How can you see anything if you have died?

I . . . I . . . don't believe I have died . . . I'm not with . . . I'm not with the body lying there on the bed.

You can see your body?

Yes. This has happened to me before, like a dream . . . being free of the body.

Is your body alive or dead?

I didn't care. I'm free. I feel like I have my wings and yet it feels like my mind and my thinking is in all of my limbs at the same time. I feel like I can see with my feet. I feel like I can see everything at once. My whole being feels like my head alone felt before. Before I thought with my mind. Now every part of me thinks.

What was the transition to this state like for you?

A very, very light feeling . . . like a change of the wind. Like the wind changed directions and I went with it instead of fighting against it.

Were there any voices? Was anyone calling your name?

No. I felt very lonely, but this was only temporary. It was my choice to be by myself. I want only one person to see me, after a while. Ann. I feel her waiting for me in the corner of the top of the room, somewhere through the ceiling, perhaps just above the house. Yes, outside the house, I know she is there waiting for me.

* * * * * *

A man, age twenty-four, Roman Catholic:

I keep going under, I can't stay afloat. God, it hurts. I come from a land of olive trees, a dry country. I'm dying and I think of my home and my wife. My wife has dark hair and olive skin. I keep getting water . . . I'm looking down and see my body floating, face down. I have died. I'm moving away from the place of my body, moving to the mainland, to my home. I know she is going to cry. I feel so peaceful. I move down and touch her cheek, but she cannot feel it. There's such peace, but I don't want to leave her because I know she is going to need me.

Do you try to make any contact with your wife other than brushing her cheek?

I try talking to her, but she can't hear me.

* * * * * *

A woman, age seventy. Episcopalian/Presbyterian:

My throat is tight, I am choking.

Now you have died.

I see my old bones there on my old bed.

How can you see your body if you have died?

I got out of it and now I'm light, light and floating.

It is better than when you had a body?

Oh, yes. Lightweight, like a young girl.

And can you see your body down below?

Yes. Old and black, all dried up. Nothing but an old woman with the mouth hanging open.

What will you do now that you have crossed over?

I want to find my daughter. I want to tell her that I love her. I needed to love more in that lifetime. I didn't love enough. I want to find her and tell her now.

* * * * * *

A woman, age thirty, Jewish:

I died when I was twenty-one.

What was the cause?

The plague . . . it was the plague. Everyone is getting sick. It's wiping out almost the whole town.

And you caught it also?

I was burning up. My mother and my two younger brothers got it, too. I was the first one to go.

Did anyone die after you in your family?

Oh, yes, a lot of them followed. Only one was left. My sister.

Did you know you were going to die?

Yes, I remember thinking only the good die young, and I was young.

What was it like for you?

I had trouble breathing. I was burning up. My body felt like it was dividing . . . just like an axe was coming down and dividing me. My body stayed and I shot off into the clouds. I wasn't interested in my body anymore.

* * * * * *

A man, fifty, agnostic:

Are you still alive at twenty-two?

No. I die, all people die.

How did that happen?

Ground shake, make hole in the ground.

Tell me about it.

It happen very quickly. We all run, no place to go, all ground shake very hard. Ground break, take some my people. Water take some people. I die with father. We go into the ground with something very hot cover our bodies . . . do not know but it look hot like fire.

Go to the moment after you died.

Don't know, just new peace. My father and my people, we go in different ways. I talk to my father several times.

As a spirit?

Yes, he helped me to understand this new life.

What did he tell you?

He says this life is more quiet than the last. We do not have to worry about food . . . drinks . . . cold or hot. Always calm, always peaceful.

How did you feel?

Feel very comfortable in this new life.

* * * * * *

Man, age forty-two, atheist:

What happens now that you have died?

I begin to float . . . separation and floating. I'm floating all over. I feel so content.

Where do you go?

Out into the light, where it is warm. I am a spirit now. I am allowing myself just to be. I feel really free and loved by something much greater than myself . . . something that I am part of.

* * * * * *

Man, age twenty-seven, uncertain religious upbringing:

Go right to the time of your death. How did it happen?

Car accident. I can see it. It was icy and I spun like a top. I hit a pole and was instantly dead.

Were you aware at that moment that you had died?

No, all I knew was that I lost control of the car.

How did you know you had died?

My body could not move. I was outside of it and I . . . my mind was alive and I went over to my physical body and could see the broken pole, the mangled metal, my bleeding body. But it's all right. It's peace now.

You felt peace?

Yes. Contentment for the first time.

Did you ever think that death would be like this?

No. When I was alive I was afraid to die. I'm not afraid anymore. I'm not afraid.

*   *   *   *   *   *

Here are some comments from people who have attended workshops and participated in regressions:

1. I was dead but I felt even more alive than when I had a physical body. It was certainly leaving the physical and going into a lighter kind of vibration. I went back and saw my body in the coal mine where I died.

2. It was like I was going into a different universe. Everything was softer, and yet more intense at the same time.

3. It was so beautiful and peaceful. I don't have any fear of death now.

4. It was like I was giving birth to myself, through the head. I slipped out with no effort at all . . . an easy delivery. I floated above, as though gravity didn't affect me at all, and time seemed to have no meaning either.

5. I thought of my daughter and how I would miss her. I felt sorry and sad, and then all of a sudden, when the blue-white light filled me, all the sadness melted away and I felt loved. I didn't want to hold on to the people of that lifetime any more.

6. As they carried my body into the church, I kept moving down to it, trying to get back into it to see what it would feel like, but I couldn't get in it, so I gave up and just watched everyone going through the motions.

7. I wanted to tell everyone not to be sad because I was alive, but I couldn't tell them that. They only believed what they saw.

8. All my pain vanished and I felt whole again. My dead self didn't have an arm, but the new me did. I was whole and feeling really all together.

In thousands of past-life regressions to previous deaths, only one has not fit the pattern of all the others – only one was different.

Let us go to the moment of death.
I'm lying in a room, not feeling very well. I'm feeling weaker and weaker, and everything stops.
What is it like, the very moment you die?
Everything just stops.
Do you have any awareness that you have died?
Everything just stops. No awareness at all.
You have no awareness of leaving your body?
None at all.

Why was this one so different? As an experiment I asked an intelligent and thoughtful person who knew nothing of my work to *pretend* to experience a past-life regression – to fake it. Working only from imagination, this woman fabricated a dramatic story, the ending was that 'everything just stops'.

Obviously, it does not come close to the real experience of death, as attested to by thousands of people who have remembered what death was really like.

15

THE WORLD BETWEEN

Hereafter, in a better world than this,
I shall desire more love and knowledge of you.

WILLIAM SHAKESPEARE, *AS YOU LIKE IT*

Between birth and death there is life, and between death and birth there is also life. Although the dimensions of this other life are different, it is every bit as real as the one we perceive through our senses and our conscious minds. In regressions, people frequently describe death as a shift in awareness, and the afterlife as a focusing of this new awareness. Few people refer to the experience of death as in any sense an ending; on the contrary, their feelings are of expansion – becoming more rather than less.

Descriptions of these experiences are consistent, case after case, the only difference being in the degree of eloquence with which people attempt to translate them into understandable terms. Words often prove inadequate, as they have been created to describe the three-dimensional world of which we are a part. Still, for most people, the after-death state is a fulfilling one. There is the sensation of filling the universe, embracing all creation, touching the essence of everything seen and unseen, becoming all knowledge, and perceiving truth beyond cultural limitations.

So grounded are we in the concepts of time and space that we have difficulty comprehending the dimensions of a non-time, non-place existence. Automatically we think of the Soul plane as a separate and distinct place quite apart from the earthly realm with a linear time frame much like our own. It requires no small effort to conceptualize fluid time and elastic space.

It is a supreme task for the rational mind to imagine the Soul plane as a different vibration from the physical plane we know (like two different tones on a tuning fork), yet even the most scientifically dogmatic people have spoken of the world between in those terms.

In the world between, free of the constraints of time and space, we can be anywhere instantly just by thinking it. To wish, to desire, to need, is to have. Perception, unfiltered by the senses and brain, becomes reality without the usual time delay experienced on the earth plane. On this plane we often wait a long time for what we want, and then sometimes we fail to recognize it when it materializes; our perception lags behind the manifestation of that which we desire. This is not so on the Soul plane, where the creative process operates outside the constraints we take for granted. These constraints include not only time and space, but also the judgemental ones of moral systems.

It can be said that on the Soul plane we become thought itself. Thoughts are felt throughout the whole being rather than just in the head, as we saw in some of the regressions of the last chapter. In altered states of consciousness during the earth life we sometimes feel that we are thinking with the whole body, but consciousness dispels the feeling. In other dimensions of life, however, thought arising throughout the entire self is the only kind possible. Further, there is no distinction between existence and experience, or between experience and thought. The following transcription is just one of many that touches on this.

Where did you go when you left the body?

Through a door, into a place that was light and full of flowers.

Was there anyone there that you knew?

Not at first, the very first, but then there were. They call themselves
guides and they were all soft colours. They spoke without moving

their mouths. They just seemed to think the ideas and I knew what they meant. I understood with my whole body.

Did you go anywhere?

I followed a path.

Where did it lead?

It was a white path, glowing white, like most everything, and it took me to another level of understanding. I seemed to know more when I followed that path.

For most people, just after crossing over there is a continuing feeling of tangible form, an awareness of arms, legs, hands, and feet that seem to be solid and transparent at the same time. If these physical features are still perceived by the individual, they are felt to be alive with thought. The feeling of form diminishes with acceptance of the different focus.

Awareness then seems to progress to a more refined state, and we perceive ourselves as pools of intense light energy. This is a natural progression for all beings, though some may need longer on the Soul plane for this stage to occur. It is often described as an intense light with a pulsating quality, or as a surging in and out of existence. The following transcript presents this often-repeated remembrance.

I seemed to be gathering energy from the universe. I was losing form after a while and . . . but I felt I had a form . . . it was real, very real to me and to others . . . but my arms and legs seemed to draw in and, as they did, I grew larger, wider, fading in and out like a pulse of blood, sort of surging like blood everywhere at once . . . but very bright white light. I'm tapping into something bigger, stronger, vaster than I am. I can't really see it, but I know it is all around me. I am secure with it round me. I seem to need this stronger form for sustenance, to survive. It's a direct tap-in, like being plugged into a high-voltage line without the jolt. I feel really loved.

In numerous sessions a comparison has emerged between the after-life and the world of dreams, and there are some striking similarities. In dreams we are able to be anywhere in an instant; past, present, and future have no real meaning and all time is simply now. In dream as in the afterlife, we are able to communicate with those who are alive and with those who have crossed over. The whole process is perpetual communication leading to growth, understanding, and sharpened perception of life at all levels.

Like experiences between lives, we forget dreams easily. Even though much may have been accomplished through the experience, if we do not awaken during, or just after, the dream we will have forgotten the scenario. In consciousness we tend to think of dreams as fantasies imposed on us from outside ourselves, yet we know that we are the creators of our dream world, just as we are the creators of our waking world.

The analogy of dreams and the world between is carried further by some individuals, who point out that thousands of nights of dreaming alternating with wakeful consciousness fill such earthly life, just as the time between lives and the lives themselves alternate to comprise the total Soul experience.

In sleep the awareness leaves the physical limitations of rational thought and freely explores whatever will promote growth. There is no concern for the physical body that sleeps – to the dreaming self the physical body does not exist. It has ceased to be; the focus has shifted elsewhere. On the earth plane we are not able to maintain two focuses at once, though there may be some shifting back and forth to satisfy needs for security, curiosity, and expanded vision. Nothing that is outside of focus really matters, and the same can be said of the Soul plane from the point of view of the earth plane.

Language differences between the waking mind and the sleeping mind are also analogous to those between each consciousness and that of the world between. The expressions of dreams and the communications within them often challenge us to interpret accurately what we have experienced. Numerous interpretations can emerge from one dream because of the language barrier that exists between levels of awareness. Just as dreams have their own language, so does the afterlife state. Generally it is non-verbal, though the need for verbalization does sometimes occur. Communication with those left behind is most often expressed as emotional energy transfer that the receiver gets as a vague hunch, an intuitive insight, or a symbol translated into words. There is always the possibility of misinterpretation. Understanding someone who is speaking the same language is sometimes difficult, and trying to interpret a different set of symbols transmitted by a different form of energy certainly increases the possibility of error.

Just as our feelings at bedtime sometimes set the stage for dreams, so the world between is coloured at first with the emotions felt just before death. Gradually these emotions fade away and are replaced by strong feelings of unconditional love. Ultimately we all operate on the frequency of love at a non-emotional level, but for many the transition from possessiveness and resentment is not easy. Moving into unconditional love means becoming more completely unified with the Divine Mind, with the universe, and the necessity of returning to the earth plane ends when the Soul achieves this complete unification. The following transcription reflects some transitions along this path.

When I decided not to stay with my body anymore, it was like I got filled with light. I started glowing and moving away and my sister was waiting for me. She told me not to be afraid and I said that I wasn't afraid at all, just peaceful and free of the awful pain. I was surprised a little at her serenity because she was always so hyper. But now she was just so peaceful and calm. It's as though you become like the person you are with, just automatically. And then I realized I was seeing and hearing with my whole body and I was expanding then, too. It felt as though I were being pumped up with helium like a balloon. I was light and inflating and it felt so good, not like the bloated feeling I'd had when I was sick, but a light, free feeling. I understood about my husband and knew the children would be all right without me. All that sadness and concern about leaving them was just swept out of me and I knew it would be OK. I had to go on and become whatever the energies around me wanted me to be.

What do you mean by the energies around you? Were there people besides your sister?

Some energies were vaguely like people . . . like people that had lost their form or shape, but were still there somehow . . . like when you know someone is looking at you. But it felt good because it was loving. My sister was still the way I remembered her, before the accident, but these other people . . . I don't know who they really were . . . were more like energies that supported and encouraged me. I was in contact with all of them and I didn't ever have to try.

The question often is asked whether we have continuing awareness of the earth plane after what we call death. It seems to depend upon whether we wish to maintain any sort of contact. Many Souls apparently spend considerable time with loved ones – guiding, guarding, urging, and advising through intuitive channels. Some decide to become teachers, and loyally fill this role for a particular person or group. One person recalled this:

I went into a valley . . . I didn't expect to be in such a beautiful place, I was led there it seems . . . and the guide said 'This is the valley where the spirits live close to the earth. You can rejoice. You can follow me or stay in the valley.' This is what I chose to do, since it was so beautiful.

One person, born most recently in 1945, described the events of the earth from 1890 to 1945 – a time when he was in the world between – as though they had happened in a few moments. His view was similar to that of a satellite passing over the earth at an elevation of fifty to a hundred miles. The comments on the latter years of the period are fascinating because they incorporate sensory details as well as intuitive awareness of several major historical events, including the drought of the 1930s and the Holocaust of World War II.

Great clouds of dust are rising and sweeping across the land below me like a great blizzard. There is anger sweeping the land, too, but across a much larger surface. It is blacker and more dangerous. It is growing more and more intense. Oh, my God, there is fire now and the noise of the explosions, two of them, and great clouds rising towards me. The anger is all resolved now for a while, and I know that it is time for me to be born again.

*　*　*　*　*　*

Another person expanded on the process of planning to re-enter the earth plane.

What is it like for you now?

I don't know if words could explain it. It was as if there were no restrictions placed on me. I was in another place of sorts . . . and yet not really . . . in another time . . . bright lights, white lights . . .

Did you go back to see your brother?

No.

So you completely let go of the physical reality?

Yes.

Did you see anyone else who had crossed over at that time?

No.

You were there by yourself?

Yes.

What was life like on the spirit plane?

It was nice. No hunger, no pain, no need for anything. I was able to see what was going on on earth. It was as if I was away from the earth, somewhere else, flying high above. In the white light . . . becoming it.

What could you see happening on earth?

People being with each other, children playing, people working.

Did you feel any need to return to the earth plane?

Yes. I hadn't done anything. I needed to do something meaningful.

How could you tell it was time to be reborn?

It was as if someone said it was my time to come back, but that I had a choice. I could choose the time . . . the date and year.

How did you find the right body?

There were two married people, two beautiful people who loved each other, and I thought to myself what kind of a child they could have. She was with child, and I entered.

At what point of development of that child did you enter?

Before she even knew she was pregnant.

So it was at the very beginning, right after conception?

Yes.

Had you considered other possible parents?

Yes. I had several choices in mind. It was up to me.

What made you reject the others?

There was something special about these two people. The others would have made good parents, but these two people were very special.

Were there other possibilities within the same culture?

No, they were all different in some way.

*   *   *   *   *   *

Another person talks about choosing parents:

How long were you on the spirit plane?

A couple of centuries, but it seemed like only a few minutes . . . no, it didn't even seem like that. It is hard to relate it to time at all.

When were you born again?

In 1610, in Denmark.

Did you know you were going to be born in Denmark?

Oh, yes, I was very much aware. It was part of the choices I had to make, an assessment of all the conditions. That's where my parents were at the time. I liked the feeling I had, but I knew I was taking on a great challenge because they were like other parents I had had many times before. I had known my father before.

Some of the conditions that make incarnations acceptable include the need to be with those we have been with in other lives. it is important for us to realize that there is no interruption in relationships when there is desire to continue them, even though the form of one or both Souls has changed. Many people have reported continuing communications with those left behind on the earth.

*   *   *   *   *   *

There is no loneliness on the Soul plane. Some people need the support of other Souls after crossing over, while others seem to prefer solitude. The following case typifies the indifference of some to having others around them.

Did you see other Souls?

Occasionally.

Did you have any desire to be with them?

Not really.

Did you want to know about the people left behind?

I tried, but was not too successful in communicating with them. I knew what was happening [to them], but that faded except for interest in John. I was never out of range with him.

Were you able to talk to others who had crossed over?

Yes . . . those most interested in learning.

How long did you remain on the Soul plane?

A long time . . . no, not really a long time. It was not long enough in some ways.

Why is that?

Because you can have whatever you want just by wishing it.

What did you want?

To be comfortable, warm, to learn whatever I desired.

And you were learning?

Oh, yes, very much.

How did you know it was time to be born again?

When I thought I had gained enough to contribute to man. Just seemed that it would be good to be with people again.

How does it feel when you are going to be in human form again?

All my energies were pulled together . . . all my energies, but I felt some fear . . . I was concerned, not afraid . . . I was concerned that

I needed more knowledge. I was concerned about trying again.

When were you born?

Nineteen thirty-one.

So you spent 120 years in the Soul plane?

Yes.

*   *   *   *   *   *

The way of communicating among Souls in the world between is made clear in the following excerpt from a session. This woman, age thirty, had no knowledge of metaphysical matters when she experienced this regression.

Where did you go after you died?

I stayed on a plane above it . . .

Above what?

The body.

How long did you remain there?

It's hard to tell . . . time . . . what is time? A day or two, I would guess, but that is only a guess.

Where did you go from there?

To be with friends.

I see. Were you able to communicate with them?

Yes.

How did you do that?

Well, we didn't have mouths. We just thought to each other.

Could you see your friends?

In a manner of speaking.

Could you see people on earth, see them doing anything?

Yes, but I had no particular desire to contact any one.

Even when you first crossed over?

Well, I did then, but that fades after you get used to a new kind of existence.

Whom did you communicate with on the Soul plane?

Some relatives, some friends, some people I had forgotten about.

Did you speak to your father and mother?

Yes.

How did you feel about your father?

All the resentment was gone, if that's what you mean. I accepted him and felt love, because I understood for the first time who he really was.

Who was he?

Someone I had been with many times before. We had things to work out that I was not aware of when I was in bodily form.

* * * * * *

Through the hypnotic regressions of many subjects it has become clear to me that the Soul plane is an infinite sea swarming with activity. On that plane there are also infinite possibilities for experience; general categories might include advising, teaching, observing, evaluating, researching, studying, and learning.

When the initial confusion and indecision of crossing over subsides, decisions are made. In many ways the early period is like a midplane of existence – a rest area – where communications among loved ones occur easily, and visitations to those still on the earth plane are made during hours of sleep. This is a time of full examination and evaluation of the whole spectrum of experiences. Guidance is given automatically to those who are confused during this adjustment to a new frequency.

Eventually everyone becomes involved with several basic issues: deciding on another return to the earth plane, entering another system of probabilities that does not include reincarnation, or recreating past lives and making adjustments to them. Those with a strong need for organized direction will choose reincarnation and the time structure it imposes. Those who have grown beyond the need for imposed structure can make a choice among intuitive possibilities that provide unlimited vistas.

We must realize that, even on the Soul plane, many levels of growth are possible. As we gain new awareness, more choices become available to us. A wise person has said that the main reason for going to college is to learn how much there is that we do not know. The same holds true for the metaphysical world, as each new insight opens us to still greater potentialities. How perfect for the human Soul, which thrives best on growth and creativity.

16

PERCEPTIONS OF THE GREATER SELF

> Most people live, whether physically, intellectually, or morally,
> in a very restricted circle of their potential being. They make use of
> a very small portion of their possible consciousness and of their
> soul's resources in general.
>
> WILLIAM JAMES, *THE LETTERS OF WILLIAM JAMES*

Only by transcending the ego-self and all its personality masks can we clearly perceive reality. This clear perception is essential for the experience of happiness; it is the distorted view of rational consciousness and/or the emotional self that creates turmoil and pain. The Greater Self or Soul is the vehicle through which we are able to gain this objective view of reality. Experience has shown that the most direct and dramatic healings of mind and body result from a communication with the Greater (Objective) Self. This Soul-source unleashes unimagined power.

Hypnosis, either self-induced or directed, is the usual mechanism by which contact with non-physical dimensions of the Self is made. In an altered state of consciousness (such as that achieved through hypnosis, meditation, or prayer) interference from the ego (Subjective Self) is reduced or eliminated, so that understandings bypass normal thought centres and are deeply felt to be truth. One client, using visual images, described the beginnings of communication with his Greater Self in this way:

I felt as if I was stepping out of the stream of thoughts that were always rushing over me, around me, through me, and I stepped out onto the bank – getting some distance from this constant flow of thoughts. And I could sit on the bank, removed kind of, just watching all the thoughts going by and not touching me, and not interested in knowing what they were all about. I was open, ready to listen to what came into me from somewhere else (above me, it seemed like). It is a kind of a funnel that starts to pour things into me and I just sit there as it comes in. I don't know what's going to be [said] next. I don't really care since I know it will help me some way. I do miss some of it because I am really getting off and just sitting on the riverbank in the warm sun with this funnel thing pouring into my head and I don't have to do anything.

Later he added, smiling,

I guess this whole process appeals to me because I'm lazy by nature, and with this I don't really have to do anything but let it happen.

Allowing the Greater Self to take over is the key to success. Letting go, combined with the belief that it will work, promotes meaningful communication, while fear and disbelief interfere with the process. Many people fear being passive because they have been taught that it makes them vulnerable and is therefore dangerous. If the client in the example had tried to maintain awareness, he could have hindered the flow of information, which in this particular session provided interesting insights into past-life connections with his girl friend.

Into everyday life, when we find the conscious mind going into neutral, we gain insights into seemingly unsolvable problems. Most of the greatest discoveries and inventions in history have resulted from a moment of *non-thought* when the Greater Self was allowed to speak its clear perceptions. The historical giants responsible for these advancements have generally been unable to describe the awareness that filled them with wisdom in an instant, but they all recognize that their inspiration was beyond the scope of their daily thoughts.

Defining the Greater Self is like trying to define electricity. It is an energy force – a pool of intense, focused energy which radiates like a sun, giving birth and nourishment to all of its earthly creations. It is the Focus Self, the sum and more of all earthly selves, past, present, and future. It may be called the Essence of Soul or the Objective Oneness of each total personality. Like the hub of a wheel with spokes extending out to the rim, the Greater Self is the nucleus around which all extensions are created.

In a sense, the Greater Self is also like the nucleus of an atom, a basic form in the universe: there is a centre around which smaller particles revolve, held in position by a dynamic energy force. The circulating particles cannot exist without the nucleus, just as a moon cannot exist without a planet, and as planets cannot exist without a sun. Blocking the energy flow from the Greater Self, like blocking the energy of the Sun, reduces the chances for survival. Attunement to this energy fills us with a never-ending supply of strength, direction, hope, and joy. Without recognition of it we despair and decline, and although we may survive, we do not truly live. Through meditation, self-hypnosis, prayer – even through sleep and some forms of exercise – we affirm the existence and importance of this energy bond. It is a subtle communication we label as well-being and intuition. Recognizing and utilizing our free access to wisdom, patience, and unconditional love sets us free, and we triumph over the challenges of daily living.

Clinically speaking, a person operating in the Greater Self mode regularly gains specific information falling into the following general categories:

1. Past lives, future lives
2. Relationships with others
3. Life themes
4. Karmic responsibilities
5. Strengths and weaknesses in character
6. Choice of parents

7. Latent creative abilities
8. Directions for the future
9. Nature of personal and universal reality
10. Historic perspectives
11. Destructive thought patterns
12. Illnesses and disabilities
13. Present problems

Unlike the ego-self (which could also be called the focus personality) the Greater Self experiences no threat to survival, no compulsion to win anything (attention, approval, love) from others, no obsessive pursuit of gratification beyond universal laws, so there are no power plays. Universal laws, few and simple as they are, form the basis for the existence of the Greater Self and the unconditional love that infuses this powerhouse of energy and all of its physical manifestations.

God, the Universal Source, permeates each Greater Self with abundant high energy, which the Self then channels into each of its ego-selves; we are nurtured by these dynamic life forces.

Focus personalities in various historical periods – our past, present, and future selves – are simultaneously in communion with the Source, but many of these selves are closed to this ever-present flow. They are the selves that are most troubled and desperate, feeling the overwhelming effects of helplessness and hopelessness.

We have always come the closest to describing the Greater Self with the word *conscience*. It is the voice of restraint, of moderation, of consideration; it forces its way into our reality through the emotion we label guilt, which can trigger fear. This is a last resort when communications on more subtle levels of our awareness have been ignored.

Sometimes people who wish to be hearing the clear, patient voice of the Greater Self confuse it with the voice of impatience and fear procuded by their own imaginations, then wonder whether to follow the directives they hear. There is a simple way to distinguish between the Greater Self and the survival-oriented self, and that is to see the degree of loving that comes through.

For most people who enter counselling to resolve a particular problem, reaching the Greater Self becomes a most rewarding expereince that saves both time and money for the client. I have seen many cases of laborious struggle in forms of therapy that tenaciously pursue 'proven' methods of interaction and avoid any metholodology that even hints at other dimensions of the Self. The being must be included in the therapy process if it is to succeed, for an ignoring of any one part is an ignoring of the whole. Lack of effective communication is the essence of personal problems, even world problems, and this communication must be seen as a vertical one to higher dimensions of self as well as a horizontal one to other people and other nations.

There is no guesswork when the Greater Self speaks during a session. The heart of the matter is laid open and speculation is laid to rest. Unfortunately, not every client is willing to accept the concept of the Greater Self, and so the process must unfold slowly until some level of belief allows the exploration. Most often this belief evolves from a past-life exploration or from simple stream-of-consciousness dialogue while in a hypnotic state. People are usually surprised that they have uttered words of wisdom, gems of insight that they could not consciously have formulated. The amazement is usually eclipsed by intense interest in the information which shows the way to future action.

When the time comes – and for some who seek a direct communication with the Greater Self it is the very first session – I guide the subject into the deepest possible level of hypnosis and ask whatever responses, images, symbols, hunches, come to mind to be expressed. There must be no editing, filtering, or blocking. *Everything* must be stated as though it were, in fact, vital information. Self-consciousness, our most persistently dogmatic element, sometimes encroaches and must be banished. Patience, encouragement, direction, and acceptance pave the way for the client to allow the Greater Self to emerge.

Most clients' Greater Selves speak haltingly at first, often sounding as if punctuation were irrelevant. There is usually a voice change, and sometimes it is very dramatic. Some Greater Selves speak eloquently with little questioning, while others wish to be asked very specific questions. All respond with the same clarity and wisdom, regardless of the conscious mental abilities of the subject. IQ has nothing to do with Greater Self wisdom.

As the person becomes more and more accustomed to simply letting the communication flow out, it becomes easier and usually more detailed. Sometimes the Greater Self wishes to be called a certain name, but most of the time there is no concern for something as concrete as a name. In fact, names are regarded by some Greater Selves as irrelevant, and that comment is fairly common. Any designation related to specific times, places, or names is not easy for the Greater Self, since they are earthly constructs.

For most people, the information comes as words through them. Some report symbols that must be translated later, while others have hunches or feelings that easily translate into words. Some have strong visual images, while others have none. The more analytical the person is in daily life, the more likely it is that the communication will be in words rather than images.

Nearly all clients, even those with years of experience in allowing the Greater Self to speak through them, are at a loss to explain what is happening or to describe the mechanisms involved. Some experience feelings of electrical energy shifts in the brain, some feel a sensation like tingling through the limbs, some have changes in temperature. Some note a rising into the awareness, and others describe a sensation of something lowering to them. All feel that a connection is made and material 'just flows in'.

The following examples of communications with the Greater Self illustrate the diversity of responses that are successful. Each example represents several of the categories of information listed earlier in this chapter. None of these people came to the Alternative Therapies Council with the intention of getting in touch with their Greater Self; the communication evolved out of past-life work or general discussions of life problems.

Past Lives

I would like to know how many lifetimes you have had on earth?

Thirty-two.

When have these occurred?

At various periods in history.

And when was your very first incarnation?

In Atlantis.

Can you tell me, give me a listing, of all the times you have incarnated?

Not all at once.

Give me a chronological listing, please.

Life may come chronologically but it is not felt chronologically. I can tell life as I feel life.

Well, how many lifetimes did you have in Atlantis?

Three.

Where did you incarnate after Atlantis?

In the desert, in Africa.

And what did you look like? White or black?

Brown.

Man or woman?

A man. Oh, the sun and the heat . . .

How did you survive? What did you do for food?

Barter.

With whom did you barter?

Other tribesmen . . . for fruit.

You used fruit for your barter?

Yes.

And what did you get in return?

Milk and bread.

What are you called in this incarnation?

Ra . . . just sounds like Ra.

Do you have a wife?

Yes, and four children.

How is your day occupied?

Moving from place to place. The desert is so big.

Do you have any animals?

Yes. Two donkeys, some horses, that's all.

How do you have fruit if you live in the desert?

There are places with water and fruit trees.

What kind of animals does the milk come from?

Goats.

You have goats?

No, I get milk from the people who have goats.

All right, you may leave that lifetime and look over the others and tell me where else you have incarnated.

In Greece and Rome.

Can you tell me about them?

It is strange to look at two lives at one time.

Which one is more interesting for you to look at?

The one in Greece. I was a doctor.

Some of your stays on the Soul plane seem to have been long ones.

Yes, hundreds of years, but a few of them have been short.

What determines the period of time between lives?

The success of the learning.

How is it possible to learn anything from a lifetime in Egypt that is filled with so much suffering? [presented in earlier session]

Many things come from that kind of a life, many things . . . endurance, patience, many things. it seems mundane, it seems worthless – but the soul learns many things.

What would you compare lifetimes to?

In a way, like a classroom, with each life like a course of study with different things to be learned. But you assess more than in school, and the classroom is so small compared to what you learn.

Does everyone on the Soul plane have an awareness of what has been learned in each lifetime?

Yes, in the Soul plane.

So, even people who seem oblivious to life in their incarnation do have an awareness on the Soul plane?

Definitely.

Does intelligence have any bearing on the matter?

None whatever. Intelligence is only a tool and nothing more.

What creates a child prodigy – like Mozart, for example?

Carry-over from a previous life or lives. Very definitely, in his case.

Why is learning retained with some of us and not with others?

It's part of the karma of the person. It is meant for that person to live a particular kind of life and he will carry over only what is necessary to live it as all people must.

Do animals have souls?

They do, but they are not on the same plane as people. They exist in what is like a family of Souls, separate from human souls. But then we are all part of the same creation.

How about planets?

The, too. All living things – stones, inanimate objects – are alive and have souls too, but they are not unique souls going through incarnation and retaining their uniqueness. Again, it is a family where some of the individual identity is lost on the return.

Can a person ever reincarnate as an animal?

No. There is no crossing of energies.

As a Soul Entity, can you describe God to me?

You have not the knowledge to understand God. The closest I can come to your understanding is to say that God is an energy, a force, a presence. It has always been a consciousness. God is many things. There is no real way to describe God. Look at your poets who have tried. God is all things.

HISTORICAL PERSPECTIVE

Can you give me the time frame for Atlantic and its location?

Persisience will accomplish much. Time was perceived to be millennia before your time reference. Time might be described for beings in Atlantis in reference to major cataclysmic events that are recorded in geological . . . by geological reference. One cataclysmic event recorded might be described as pressure so greatly magnified that the earth structure was broken. This was caused by the beings of Atlantis annihilating their own physical probabilities, and their reality was destroyed. This caused great havoc on your earth. Geology records this event. My perception of what you call time makes this event happen long before your marking of time. You mark time differently than the beings of Atlantis marked time, but in your time reference, this occurred about eight million years ago. With regard to location, it was southerly from you, located beneath the equator nearer to the South Pole. But your South Pole was the North Pole to Atlantis, which makes the poles reversed according to your perception. So they felt they were located toward the top of the world. When the beings of Atlantis annihilated themselves, they caused the earth to shift poles instantly, which caused much havoc in the earth.

Was there an Atlantis?

Oh, yes. There was much advancement.

In what terms?

In areas of science and medicine, and human growth potential. The world today is only beginning to learn science. Human growth potential they lost, after being so close. The development of the spirit was neglected. It was a matter of priorities. It's much, much more important that we grow spiritually. We can conquer all things through spirit. They destroyed themselves because they misused the powers of their minds. It was devoid of spirituality. It was just straight mind warfare that even affected the crust of the earth.

LIFE THEMES, KARMIC RESPONSIBILITIES

I would like you to look over various lives and tell me what patterns have been set up.

One for elevated consciousness, one through experiencing as many factions of humanity as possible, to unify the one Soul through experiencing the many.

What can the person through whom you speak learn in this lifetime? What is this lifetime meant to be?

Patience, humility, inner strength, inner resources.

Is she succeeding?

Yes.

What is your best direction for her in her relationship with her husband and children?

To get the most out of her interaction with them, to experience them fully, not to isolate again.

So she isolated herself in past incarnations?

Yes. She must risk exposure because of fear of loss in the past. This is very important. She can identify with others and still maintain her own unique awareness.

How many lives have you sparked?

Forty-two.

Does any one lifetime stand out as part of the pattern your remarks have suggested?

Yes. One life that was a great spiritual growth, but through isolation, and in that lifetime there was death by torture. It was near Jerusalem.

Because of religious belief?

Yes. Much trepidation and holding back resulted. Fear of violence, fear of speaking her own mind resulted. Fear must be removed. It has to be out of the way, so that the being can venture forth to new growth experiences. Mor could have been gained from the other experiences had fear not gotten in the way. Stumbling blocks that are self-imposed just waste time. There are enough of them without creating any.

You mentioned a lifetime as an Indian. How did that follow the fear theme?

There was no commitment to the girl he loved. He stayed with the responsibility for the mother and sister, responsibility that should have fallen to the older brother.

So unwillingness to assume responsibility is part of that fear?

Yes, most definitely.

In the Jerusalem lifetime, was that at the time of Jesus?

After. It was part of the pattern.

What advice would you give to the being through whom you speak for future direction?

As in all of you, physical-level discipline is an important, important step now. The rest falls in line. The overeating is fear too, for food buffers the outside energies.

RELATIONSHIPS

Has the being been with her husband in the past?

Yes. There was a monastery in the Alps, French Alps. They worked together. Lots of snow there. They're writing, producing scriptures.

This is a significant life then?

Yes. They are working together on a mutual effort. It is important that they support each other in their work, then and now. It was the beginning of a bond.

How about the daughter and the hostility she shows?

It's jealousy.

Jealousy of what?

Of the father. She [the daughter] knew him first.

Before the monastery time?

Yes. They've been sisters. They are in competition now.

And the daughter is feeling that now?

Yes, a competition from the past.

How should this being involve this competition?

Just step aside when they are together and allow it to be. It really doesn't matter because they've been together all along anyway, and they will be together more times in your future.

*   *   *   *   *   *

Were there other lifetimes with James?

Yes, in the Middle East. I was male and he was female. In Egypt I was male again, a healer, and he was a healer also. In Atlantis I was female and he was male. He was an engineer working with something very technical. I didn't understand . . . something to do with light. He was very wise. We were lovers. He was Aram and I was Alana and we were always together.

And how about the man who became this being's father in this lifetime? How does he tie in?

At the time of Alexander the Great, she was married to him. He was a simple shepherd and they had a very quiet life. They were very close. He was gone for a period of time but she always knew he would come back.

How about the woman who became a mother in this lifetime to the channel?

She was the child in one of the old cities . . . together they had to wash the clothes in the well water. She was a boy child, a beautiful child with dark hair and great big eyes.

*   *   *   *   *   *

What is the life-after death state like for you?

I am in the Light.

Where?

In the Light, the Light that I come from, the Spirit is something that comes with you and guides you. If you do not have a body, you still have a spirit. You do not need a body for Spirit. Each life experience is for learning. Some people learn very quickly, and others much slower.

When was the Indian lifetime you spoke about earlier?

It would be . . . the 1500s.

Where was it?

It was in the Caribbean. It is now called Puerto Rico.

And what was it that you were to learn in that lifetime?

Patience, tolerance for different ways of looking at things. I am still working on those two.

Did you learn anything between lives?

Yes, in peace one learns too, but most of the knowledge comes from lives on earth.

Why do you have trouble concentrating on your work in the present focus personality?

[This was the issue the client brought into counselling: 'Why can't I focus on my work and my studies? I seem to have some kind of mental block.']

Some of my relationships in early life interfere with me in many ways. My father did not know how to speak to me. Everything that I said or did, as far as he was concerned, was wrong. He was very old-fashioned, with very old ideas. He did not seem to have the understanding that life is change. To him something new was a wall and he did not know how to deal with it. Consequently he did not know how to treat me. He did not understand and he always thought of me as dumb.

Why is this barrier to your work and study just beginning to show itself now that you are in your thirties?

It has shown itself a lot of times but was not recognized. When I was young I had moments when I thought I would die because the energy in my brain was so violent. The pain was there and there was pressure too, but I tried to ignore it. Now it is recognized and so it interrupts even more. It relates to my father and I compare him at some level with my father in the Indian life and the difference makes me very sad, but that is my lesson . . . to see the best in people and not to react to their worst. I must not compare people, even people in my life who are close.

RELATIONSHIP [WITH HUSBAND] AND ILLNESSES

She [the client] must learn that pain is not necessary to learn lessons. Somewhere she has learned that pain is necessary and that is wrong. She must stop trying to rescue too. Let John's Greater Self help him and stop interfering with this. There were times when he was soaking in the tub that he wanted to cross over, and she knew that and would not release him for fear of her own guilt. Yet when he injured his foot, she ran for help and then went back. That's bothering her. She must let go of that; she could not have helped any more had she stayed and been in danger. He was violent. Those few moments in time related to that decision she made and her actions are unimportant. She did go back and help and that is what the issue is. She could reach out at the time and not be afraid of his blood as she had been in past lives.

You mentioned a problem with the liver. How does that tie into all this?

It is many-fold, going back a long, long time when she abused it. It's been weak for many lifetimes.

Give more detail, please.

There was a lifetime when she drank too much wine, and caused the liver to become very damaged. That's why now she is allergic to grapes and the wine and the reaction is so bad she must learn to throw it off in this lifetime and not keep carrying it with her. It does not serve her purpose anymore. The whole liver is reacting to guilt too, for guilt affects the liver by blocking its functions so it must be cleansed.

What other carryovers do you see besides the guilt and the relationship to John?

There is a ship, a sailing ship. She is a man and is wearing a striped shirt; there is much physical strength. The seas are very rough, there is water splashing everywhere, up over the side. There is a fight. There is a man with intense hatred. There have been fights before. In his hand is an instrument, like a heavy pipe. He strikes me in the back [ugh!]. The back is now a weak point. She instigated the attack so there is more guilt here too. Guilt for pain. Now the back is a weak point, like a space that she must put extra energy into because negativity can come through into her if she doesn't. The back is very receptive to negativity and that stress. She needs to plug it, get rid of it, and smooth it so that it no longer exists. There was another time that ties in with the back that is earlier. It seems to be an early Eastern setting.

How about the foot and the knee problem?

That is not so relevant now. They will not change in this lifetime. One step at a time. The liver is most important now. She must reject the feelings of guilt and sympathy that she has carried for John and others. And by using white light, she can best clear herself of these hurts.

By white light, do you mean universal healing energies?

Yes. She can imagine a white light, in a pulsating ball coming to her and infusing her as she accepts it. It will heal and strengthen. She should do this several times every day.

Why is the being dealing with so much suffering and pain in this lifetime?

When she came in, one lesson that she needed to learn was how other people felt. She had several lifetimes teaching on stronger and higher vibrations and lost touch with pain. She felt it necessary to feel the pain and understand people so that she may help in constructive ways in the future. It is not necessary for her to experience any more pain or to the depth that she has taken it on. She has learned the lessons of pain and now, by loving without rescuing or feeling guilty if it is not returned, she will move beyond the need for pain.

*   *   *   *   *   *

I would like you to look ahead if you would and tell me about a future life of Robert and what he can utilize of that lifetime today (since time is an illusion)?

The being Robert would like to play the piano but has felt frustrated with this pursuit. He has been learning through traditional methods with a step-by-step approach. This is wrong for him, since in a future life, as you call it, he will be a great pianist. I see him in the San Francisco of your future after the rebuilding of the city.

Rebuilding of the city?

Yes. A devastating earth movement has destroyed much of the area and Robert lost everything but his great gift of music. He . . . he . . . he had some injury to his right hand, but this does not stop him from playing. He is much in demand with the electronic form of his music.

How can Robert make use of this talent now?

By breaking with traditional learning methods. By meditating before sitting at the keyboard and drawing the future energy into him. Much of his learning can be intuitive rather than 'by the book'. He has a better ear for sound than he realizes. He can compose now – and play well.

[Robert came out of the trance smiling with the idea of composing. 'I can barely play "Mary Had a Little Lamb", let alone compose.' I asked Robert if he got any idea of the date of the future life and without thinking, he said 2085. Six months later Robert had completed the material that is normally part of a three-year course of study. He incorporated the intuitive approach with the step-by-step traditional learning methods. He was more than pleased with the breakthrough.]

*   *   *   *   *   *

Soul entity, can you tell me how many lives the person through whom you speak has lived?

One hundred and seventy-one.

How far back do these lives extend?

Before any concepts of time as you know them can be perceived.

How about the locations for the first incarnations?

These occurred on worlds that you do not know of. One place is thousands of light years from your earth. A much bigger planet, something like your Jupiter. She has always carried some portion of this first-life memory with her and it has made her feel different from others who have never experienced a different physical reality.

And many of her lives have also occurred on earth?

Yes. Many in all civilizations at all times. She has been in nearly every walk of life, from teacher to maid, from scientist to shepherd. She has been a father, a son, a mother, a daughter.

And what is it she is working on most this time around?

She is trying to take more control of thoughts. She has the tendency to allow thoughts and feelings of others to come into her and then be influenced by them. Taking control of her thoughts and feelings is the most important thing she can do. She has been too open because she has experienced so much of what she sees and feels around her. She must become more concerned about her own sense of balance and she must be less passive around others. What is right for them is not right for her. She seems to think she has a sense of control at this time. She is mistaken. She is trying to make herself believe she has this strength now, but she is exaggerating the truth of the matter. There are two numbers that are coming into focus that are a key here. They are two twos. In two years and two months by your time measurements, she will have attained a greater measure of control over her thoughts and feelings and be able to function more fully in every phase of her life. EVERY PART OF HER LIFE WILL CHANGE. She must work diligently now to make this probability occur, for it is a most fulfilling time for her.

[This client two years and six months later was in a new job that doubled her salary. She was engaged to marry a very positive and loving man. She had eliminated all food and pollen allergies. The strength did not happen overnight. She felt it evolving gradually over the period of time from the session through the next two and one-half years.]

* * * * * *

Can you tell me, Soul Entity, if any of the lifetimes were particularly important as influences on the present one?

Yes. There was one in particular where the family was poor and she felt unloved, like a burden. It was hard for her.

How far back in time are we going for this, Entity?

From this time, it was 230 years ago.

How is that lifetime affecting the entity Beatrice today?

She felt similar feelings as a child in this life and it reminded her of the unloved feelings of that life. This life triggered deeper feelings in her.

What is creating the feeling of being trapped that she talks about? She also talks about the fear of involvement with others. Can you explain that too?

The feeling of being trapped comes from several different lives, where the feelings but not the memories remain. In one life she was buried alive and tried to claw her way out of the grave. It was a horrible, suffocating panic-filled death. In another lifetime, she dies in a fire, again suffocating in the smoke, and in a lifetime in Wales, as a miner, her fear of explosion and a sealing of the mine came to pass and she died there too. She has had many lives where people have suffocated her with jealousy and protectiveness. In one life she was crippled; her father overprotected her. (That's her mother in this lifetime.) In many ways she lost people very close to her. This lifetime is no exception to this pattern that she thinks she needs to perpetuate. She is afraid of losing them, so she pushes them away. She has not learned how to love so she can be free. She either possesses or rejects, just as she has been possessed or

PERCEPTIONS OF THE GREATER SELF ～

rejected. She must break these old, repeating patterns by carrying the awareness between lives into those lives.

Has her mother shared any other lives with her?

Yes. Her mother has been her daughter and also her friend in other lives.

How about her father?

Her father has been her teacher, and a distant relative.

Is there anything you would like to add, Entity?

Beatrice knows how to proceed. The help is available to her if she just lets it come through. It is available to everyone. All they have to do is realize it is there and wanting to help them.

ON YOUR OWN
≈

Nothing can bring you peace but yourself.

RALPH WALDO EMERSON,
ESSAYS, FIRST SERIES, 'SELF-RELIANCE'

Despite the warnings that abound about the dangers of working on one's own with hypnosis, it is completely safe if certain criteria are met. Self-hypnosis is a meditative state and, like meditation, proper conditions produce the best results. If conditions are right and precautions are followed, working on one's own or with close friends can reveal insights into the past, in this lifetime and others, and open channels to the Greater Self. Sometimes these insights are as significant as those gleaned initially while working with a professional counsellor. Exploration in depth usually requires professional guidance, just as does any detailed or complex activity: Anyone can change a light bulb, but an electrician is generally needed to rewire the house! Hypnosis, like electricity, is an energy flow, and it requires many of the same precautions and preparations for safety, whether working alone or with friends.

GOING IT ALONE

If you are the type of person who accomplishes more by yourself than with others, then you may benefit by working alone with self-induced regressive hypnosis. Establishing a solid experiential base in meditative self-hypnosis can facilitate working with others later.

Indeed, there are some advantages to working alone:

1. You are able to focus your energies without the distraction of other energies around you.
2. You can establish your own rules without having to get group approval.
3. There can be no conscious or unconscious attempts to gain recognition from others, nor is self-consciousness a factor.
4. You are able to speak into a tape recorder without distracting anyone.
5. You are able to adjust your experience time according to the degree of success you are encountering.

The disadvantages of working alone are much like the disadvantages of doing anything alone. In a solitary activity one misses many of the benefits of sharing with others who are moving in the same direction. The following disadvantages of working alone should be considered:

1. There are no helpful suggestions from others.
2. You will miss the experiences of others, which often act as important learning tools.
3. Motivation for success and, more important, for consistency, is lower in most cases when working alone.
4. Multiple interpretations of the experience are unavailable.

EXPERIENCING WITH FRIENDS

In deciding to work with others toward understanding of the multi-dimensional self, the concept of 'friend' is most important. Your degree of comfort and feelings of safety are vital for success in a group setting, even if only one other person is involved, so you must really know the person or persons with whom you wish to share complex and often confusing portions of Self. You must be able to

DISCOVERING YOUR PAST LIVES

close your eyes and let the world pass you by without any anxiety about being off guard to external threats. Nothing creates anxiety and frustration faster in personal explorations than to be with people you cannot really trust because of their personal insecurities.

What traits do you look for in potential participants? Sincerity, sensitivity, patience, understanding, supportiveness, and genuine caring are most important. Even though each person in the group is exploring individually, the group itself is working on higher levels toward contractually established goals. Remember that even a one-a-month exploration group is a complex relationship on many levels, so it is important to be aware of the positive and negative potentials of such an alliance ahead of time, before the contract is made. Of course a group can dissolve and negate any spiritual contract after only one meeting, but why experience any unpleasantness or waste time with any activity that is unfulfilling, when knowing intuitively ahead of time can prevent disappointment.

If we consider a group as two to ten people, then discovering the best number of participants becomes an individual matter. You may find that working with just one other person produces much better results than getting together with five others or even three others. Again, remember that the most important consideration is the personality of the person or persons with whom you work, and the number of people is a secondary consideration.

The most successful groups, like the most successful individuals, experience a flowering of awareness as they dedicate themselves to regular participation in altered states of perception. Get-togethers may be once a week, twice a month, once a month – there are any number of possible schedules. What is important is that each participant knows when and where the experience will occur, so that adjustments can be made at all levels of being in advance. This, of course, is not done at a conscious level; the preparation occurs quite automatically. This is not to say that extemporaneous gatherings are inappropriate or unsuccessful, but they would be the exception rather than the rule.

You may find that you wish to begin your exploring alone, then move on with one other person, and gradually expand your circle until you have reached an ideal number. You can call it simply a meditation group, or a psychic exploration group, or a past-lives research association – the possibilities are many. Remember that *someone* must get the group going, and if no one is willing to take the initiative to set it up, then you must consider how strongly you wish to work with others. The point is that, if you really want to work with friends on discovering truth, you may be the one who must take the responsibility of getting the ball rolling.

Groups of from two to ten participants work best. Any more than ten requires a strong group leader who would normally retain the role for the duration of the group's existence. After a period of time, the leader will probably wish to hand over the responsibility to someone else. If more than ten people wish to participate, it would be better to form several smaller groups so that the intimacy allows each person in turn to share the guidance responsibilities.

GUIDELINES FOR SUCCESS

Whether you are working by yourself or with others, the following guidelines will ensure safe and rewarding experiences:

1. Do not ever enter a self-exploration if you are feeling fear; whether this fear be of the experience itself or of others makes no difference. You must know the people and know what you may encounter in altered states before you begin.

2. Do not work on the past if emotions of the present are strong. There will be too much colouring of the past situations and distortions of truth may result.

3. Do not work in an unfamiliar setting; explore the past from a place you know and trust. Energies differ from place to place.

4. Do not use drugs to induce past-life recall. Not only can drug reactions be unexpected and difficult to deal with, but the

material sought can be greatly distorted. Some drugs intensify sensitivity to emotional traumas – past, present, and future.

Here are some suggestions for successful experiences on your own:

1. Try to enter an altered state without expectations. Even more importantly, do not carry any expectations into the experience, since expectations are a product of the conscious mind and all conscious thoughts block altered states of awareness.

2. Be willing to accept information in whatever form it may come to you. For some people images are the vehicle for communication; for others thought forms or symbols or words seem to paint the picture. Be open to any form of communication with the past, future, or Greater Selves.

3. Body position must feel right to you, but do not assume a sleep position; never use the bed, for example, as the place for experiencing meditation or hypnosis, as it is a triggering mechanism for sleep and different brain cells are stimulated and relaxed.

4. Eliminate all present and potential distractions, like the telephone and doorbell. Such interruptions can be more than annoying; they can be startling!

5. Establish direction before beginning. If you wish to know a past-life connection with someone, for example, hold a picture of the person in your hand or in your mind and as you regress yourself or as you are guided in the group, allow the connection to become clear. The secret here is to think *with*, not *about*, the person.

6. Give yourself ways to relieve emotional stress of the past. By telling yourself that lifting a finger slightly relieves emotional pressures, you will establish a conditioned response that will be effective not only in altered states but also in everyday, waking states of stress.

7. See the experience as a learning situation, not as a moment in which you are putting your abilities on the line. Remember hypnosis, whether guided or alone, is a talent that is innately easy for some and difficult for others, but it can be learned by all.

8. Enjoy yourself, no matter how important the experience may be for you. Do not set yourself up for disappointment or frustration. Keep it light.

9. Look back with the intention of finding the key to hidden talents, positive relationships, and general knowledge about self that will help you to live more fully in the present time frame. Leave the heavy stuff for professional consultations.

10. Be patient. Positive results often take many practice sessions, especially if you are not a regular meditator.

11. Experiment with various types of background sounds and music. You may find that a particular sound will trigger you easily and quickly into an altered state. Some people do well with recordings of a single note played on some woodwind instrument. Many good meditation recordings are available, some with instructional guidance by a professional hypnotist. The Alternative Therapies Council offers several types of guided sessions on cassettes for in-home regression and Greater Self work.

12. Do not let anyone pressure you into predetermined results or, because of previous successes, expect a performance from you. Do not get into finding missing persons or pets, jewels or jaguars unless you have a proven track record and can stand the stresses of making errors amid the successes.

13. Do not let anyone discourage you from your seeking. Many people with both good and less-than-good intentions may try to thwart your efforts because they simply do not understand.

14. Do not work in altered states if you are excessively hungry or full, sleepy or excited. Stimulants like coffee, colas, and some teas can interfere with the discovery process that depends on just the right amount of relaxation.

15. Have several types of recording equipment available so that during or after a session you can easily click on a tape recorder or take a pencil in hand and make notes on your experience. Sometimes memories of such experiences fade quickly with the return of conscious awareness.

16. If you decide to research anything you experience, reread Chapter 12, 'Beyond the Shadow of a Doubt', and do not become disappointed or discouraged.

Whether you decide to work by yourself or in a small group, the following suggested activities should prove helpful as a beginning point in your explorations. There is no need to limit yourself to these, nor need you rely on only one or two techniques over a long period of time, especially if they are not producing the results you wish. Be flexible and creative in choosing your methods. Although these methods are directed to group work, most can be easily adapted to working alone.

EYE CONTACT METHOD

Place participants face to face with a partner, about three to six feet separating them. Lower the room lighting so that faces are barely visible or, better yet, use a candle or two to provide just the right amount of soft lighting. Partners do not take their eyes off each other. Persisting in this focusing triggers an open-eyed altered state of awareness that takes both participants into the past. The face of the partner seems to change, taking on different features. Mentally or physically record the feelings or impressions you have as the features change. You can identify the changes within yourself also, for your features are changing too as perceived by your partner (who is noting them down). Occasionally you will recognize your partner as a person from your past – a most gratifying experience.

AUDITORY STIMULATION METHOD

With each participant facing a wall, various sounds or types of music (especially mood music) are played. Many records and tapes are available for this method. Even a special recording can be made from a sound-effects record. Motor noises at certain frequencies can help to induce an altered state of consciousness. Single notes played by a woodwind instrument are effective, as is soft meditation music.

VISUAL STIMULATION METHOD

Many variations of this method exist; finding the right one is an exciting challenge. A group working outdoors in a country setting may wish to focus on a particular star at night, or in daylight, on a fixed point on a tree or a rock. Gazing into still waters or focusing on the sound and repetition of crashing waves at the ocean can produce the conditions that make altered states of awareness possible. Indoors, a number of visual effects can be set up: rotating discs, fixed three-dimensional patterns, flashing lights (be careful with strobe lights, since they can induce epileptic seizures in those who are prone to epilepsy), a blue light, or a flickering candle, preferably blue (blue has an effect on the electrical energy patterns in the brain), to name but a few ideas. All of the above have proved to be successful. The important consideration in visual, as in auditory, stimulation is consistency of sound or image. With sound there should be no sudden variation in the pattern, nothing unexpected that intrudes on the altered state; for visual devices, there must be consistent intensity of motion or nonmotion.

Photograph Method

A portrait photograph is circulated in the group with each person intuitively feeling some response to the person in the picture. These responses may be very vague or very specific, but no matter how they seem, they should be shared with the others in the group.

Mirror Method

With lighting at a low intensity, each person holds a mirror before him or her and focuses on the reflected image. Changes in physical features will begin to occur and they will stimulate remembrance of the lifetime of the face seen in the mirror. This technique works especially well using individual two-way mirrors so that the slight transparency allows some of the room lighting to come through. Holding the mirror out from the face in front of a plain background produces good results.

Psychometry

Touching something owned and valued by another person can sometimes trigger altered states of awareness related to the object, the owner, or oneself. The eyes are not used in this exercise – only the feelings created by touching the object.

Historical Reference Point Method

A group leader mentions a country and/or a year, giving everyone five to ten minutes to feel any sense of connection to it. After the allotted time has elapsed, another time period or country is mentioned, and so on until a half-dozen or so time periods and/or countries have been mentioned and participants have had a chance to respond within themselves and possibly to take notes on their feelings.

ROLE PLAYING METHOD

Someone in the group begins by assuming any role that feels right and each person takes on a personality that will in some way fit the role assumed by the first person. By being in a condition of psychic empathy with the leader and his or her role, you will find much understanding of past selves can emerge. Self-consciousness must be rejected in this method since it is most likely to occur in this free self-expression exercise.

STORY INSPIRATION METHOD

Inspiration for regression material can emerge from a historical story constructed extemporaneously by a group member. The story must have the key ingredients of plot-action, movement, and character – plus a physical description of a person or people (with or without names), and a setting. The story should be kept as simple as possible. Those listening in a slightly altered state of consciousness try to visualize as best they can, allowing themselves to be triggered with personal awareness of the past. Participants may find themselves leaving the storytelling and moving away along their own story lines.

EARLY EXPERIENCE TRIGGERING METHOD

Each group participant in succession tells briefly about a real personal experience of this lifetime and upon conclusion, asks the group 'What does that remind you of in your own past?' Without thinking of an answer, each person writes an automatic response according to whatever comes into his or her mind at that moment. The image or feeling may be of childhood in this lifetime or it may be of some event in the distant past. In either case, the long term memory banks will be made more accessible for further exploration. Experiences can be shared with the group after everyone has had an opportunity to present the personal story.

Focused Reading Method

Each group member makes some intuitive comment about the past of a member in the group. Whatever comes to mind, no matter how far-fetched it may seem to the conscious mind, is verbalized. Not only does surprising accuracy emerge, but many members of the group will have the very same comments!

Direct Induction Method

One person in the group can elect to be the inductor of an altered state in the other members. The person who acts as inductor should possess a soothing voice, a sense of timing, and a relaxed and patient presentation. The following transcription should be read slowly, word for word, with or without background music or visual stimulation:

> As you look to the centre of your forehead, you will find that your eyes wish to close. The lids feel heavier and heavier and you wish them to be closed. Do not strain your eyes as you focus upward; just allow your eyes to be as comfortable as your whole body is becoming with every breath you take. [Long pause: 1–2 minutes.] Let your eyes now be comfortably closed and this will help you to be more and more relaxed. Work down through your whole body now, feeling the relaxation growing with every breath. You are going deeper and deeper into relaxation. [Wait three minutes.]

I will count now and every number will help you to move away from consciousness and into an altered state of perception. One . . . two . . . On ten, you will be deeply and comfortably relaxed in an altered state of perception . . . three . . . four . . . five . . . six . . . seven . . . eight . . . By simply lifting any one of your fingers at any time, you will release any stress or emotional energies that are disturbing you . . . nine . . . ten. Now you are deeply and comfortably relaxed in an altered state of perception. [Wait one minute.] On number 15, you will pass through a tunnel and into a scene of the past [or into contact with your Greater Self]. You will be able to communicate fully and freely with the images that fill your awareness. You are directed to a meaningful experience that is positive and that will help you to better understand yourself in some way. For the moment, you will not contact a negative experience from the past. Eleven . . . twelve . . . thirteen . . . fourteen . . . fifteen. You are now in contact with your Greater Self or with a revealing scene from the past. You may feel free to move back or forward in time as you wish. When you hear me count backwards from 15 to zero, you will return to the conscious reality of the room you left behind. If you wish to return sooner, all you need to do is raise one hand slightly and you will return refreshed, focused and feeling fine. You may now continue to explore. [After 10 minutes to half an hour, count back slowly to zero in the following way:]

Fifteen . . . fourteen . . . thirteen . . . now you are leaving the altered state of perception that has provided so much insight for you . . . twelve . . . eleven . . . ten . . . nine . . . eight . . . seven . . . six . . . five . . . four . . . On zero, you will open your eyes feeling fine, focused, and refreshed, remembering everything you have experienced with great clarity. You will have no lasting negative effects from your experience. Any lingering effects will be only positive . . . three . . . two . . . one . . . zero . . . You may open your eyes.

After this kind of experience, members may wish to record their impressions and experiences or may wish to share them with the other members.

It is very important to remember that group members must be supportive of each other, encouraging innovation and individual expression. Self-consciousness can interfere with the process nearly as much as fear, so nothing in the group should condone self-consciousness or anxiety. Any feelings of friction among members, or competition expressed in attempts to control or build self-images, are totally out of place. A successful group experience is one in which each member helps all the others to better understand themselves. The end result is that each person has a clearer understanding of himself or herself as a multi-dimensional being with intuitive talents never before tapped and utilized in such a constructive way.

18

EVERYONE WANTS TO KNOW

Time dissipates to shining ether the solid angularity of facts.
RALPH WALDO EMERSON, *ESSAYS: FIRST SERIES, 'HISTORY'*

At the present time, there is much curiosity in the world about the non-physical aspects of reality. Many questions are asked over and over again as people begin to explore the boundaries of this new frontier. This chapter answers a selection of the questions that come up most frequently.

1. *Is hypnosis dangerous?*

Hypnosis is a tool and, like any tool, it can be misused – but of itself, it is not dangerous. Health professionals and trained lay practitioners are finding the therapeutic benefits of hypnosis to be greater than anyone ever suspected. The more subtle forms of hypnosis – such as those used by advertisers, by unscrupulous religious leaders, or by negative parents – are dangerous. When the subject is aware of the hypnotic process, he or she is in control.

2. *What are ghosts?*

Probably most ghosts are the product of overactive imaginations or the partial manifestations of fear fantasies. However, some ghosts are 'real' in the sense that an unquiet energy still wishes to have physical form and is unwilling to relinquish its hold on physical reality. Generally these restless beings are harmless, but they may be angry and confused. Both types seek out channels for materialization, the best ones being pubescent teens and other emotional individuals. We might call them 'old ghosts' because they have been around so long. A new ghost, by comparison, is the focused energy of a person who has just died and wishes to be   with loved ones to comfort and reassure them. A third type of ghost is a product of an out-of-body experience. People experiencing this phenomenon can partially materialize in a desired setting, thus creating a ghost-like image.

3. *What is ESP, and is there anything to it?*

ESP, or extrasensory perception, is awareness without the aid of the physical senses. It is a sensing from a different perspective, an intuitive knowing. Some of the varieties of ESP are *psychometry*, touching something and knowing its history or the history of its owner; *dowsing*, finding water or minerals with a twig or some such natural tool; *telepathy*, mind reading; *clairvoyance*, seeing the future.

It is important to realize that ESP is natural to everyone, not just a selected few; however, most people ignore it or reject it as unnatural. Despite this, we all use ESP daily. It is the most valid tool we possess for an accurate assessment of reality.

Carl Jung said about one form of ESP telepathy, 'Anyone who has the least knowledge of parapsychological material which already exists and has been thoroughly verified will know that so-called telepathic phenomena are undeniably facts'.

4. *How do you counsel the person who believes Evil to be real in the universe?*

For the person who insists that Evil is a real force that is opposed to Good, a product of the Universe, any discussion of personal control and responsibility, past-life regressions and work with the Greater Self are often very productive, although disbelief does interfere. Viewing Evil realistically, we see that it is a product of the insecure ego-self. Thus, we see that insecurity produces fear, which produces hate, which is the Evil that we confront every day. The universe could not produce Evil. It would make no sense in the scheme of creation, which is a never-ending process.

5. *I can understand the value of exploring past lives, but what good comes from looking at future lives, since they are going to happen anyway?*

Knowing what lies ahead helps us to adjust our direction. Since there are no absolutes concerning future events, but only levels of probabilities, the best we can ever do is to tune into the strongest level of probability. Knowing helps us to grow in the fastest, most direct way or to make adjustments to create a different future probability. When we consider that time is an illusion, we can see the progression (exploring the future) is just as valuable as regression (exploring the past). As hard as it is to believe, our future selves affect us as much *now* as our past selves. There is a relationship in which one part in one time frame affects all other parts in all other time frames. One Greater Self of a client stated it this way:

> *Belief is the key. When beings believe within themselves certain truths of reality, they affect the simultaneous vibrational frequency of their other personalities existing in other times, with regards to your concept of time. If one being in one reality believes in a concept, even if another personality in another reality believes the complete opposite, each belief would affect the other until one belief or the other wins the entity over to it, all other aspects of this entity (past and future selves) begin to subject themselves to the correct belief immediately. You can influence your past and future personality aspects by knowing the truth now, and all are affected now.*

6. *Do any other beings ever come through in a session?*

Sometimes a person who is sensitive to energies of other beings will channel observations of those beings. There is usually some voice change and modification of speech patterns. Usually the being will identify itself and indicate its reason for being present. Valuable insight can be gained when this happens. In one case a client was warned not to take a particular drug that her physician had prescribed a few hours earlier because of the probability of severe allergic reaction. Since she had never experienced any allergy problems in the past, she decided to take the drug anyway, but only half the prescribed dose. (She was too embarrassed to tell her physician about the knowledge she had.) Several hours after taking the drug, she was rushed to the hospital with swelling and breathing problems. Had she taken the full dosage, she may have died.

In another case, a salesman had misplaced an important set of papers. He thought they were stolen until a being, identifying itself as 'the energy that knew you when you were a child', told him to look behind the refrigerator. He recalled placing the papers on a shelf next to the refrigerator and found the papers with no difficulty.

7. *What is the best way to meditate or use self-hypnosis?*

Follow these few steps:

1. Eliminate physical distractions and insure uninterrupted safety.
2. Make the body comfortable.
3. Clear the mind of thoughts (imagine you are stepping out of the stream of thoughts into a warm, dry bank that is saturated with sunlight).
4. Become receptive, listening with the mind's ear, seeing with the mind's eye.

The Greater Self of one client said this:

Meditation does not need to be ritualized as much as most beings think, but there must be consistency in the practice. The actual method of meditation would evolve from within each being's inner self. Technique is not the most important aspect. Various positions can be used, for beings have their favourite positions for every action. What is more important than position of body is position of mind. You should follow that best position of mind and let each little thought that comes within that attitude or position of mind be focused upon. This stimulates intuitive connection with other dimensions of non-physical reality and provides clear insight into matters of concern. In other words, do not take thoughts into meditation with you, but clear the mind's slate and allow thought forms to grow after you have silenced the everyday mind. Distractions from any source, be they thoughts or external sounds, can lessen the effectiveness of the process. Most assuredly, Dear One, position of mind is the key.

8. *A few years ago, my cat, Mittens died and several months later my neighbour's cat had kittens. I picked one of the litter and discovered that this kitten was like Mittens in every way, even in the little things . . . I'm convinced Mittens has returned to me. Is this possible?*

Because of the brief time between the death of Mittens and the birth of the new cat, there was little time for you to forget Mittens. You carried a strong energy of Mittens with you, which in fact, kept Mittens very much 'alive'. The house itself contained the energy of your first cat, too. So much learning and motivation is related to energies present in an environment that the new cat could have understood, at some level, your needs and expectations. Unquestionably, animals do fulfill our needs. There is, of course, the possibility, too, that much of Mitten's Soul energy immediately invested itself in the new kitten to be with you and you recognized it intuitively. I feel that animals enter a Soul-pool of their species after death where the individual focus is gradually lost and assimilated by the Collective Soul. Mittens, or a good portion of Mittens, may have returned before a complete assimilation of the individual identity. We can think of an animal Soul as a drop of rain returning to the cloud and being absorbed into the whole cloud, part of which falls again as a new drop of rain with some of the original drop in the new one.

9. *How do you explain the Biblical Day of Judgement?*

Every day is the Day of Judgement for each one of us, since the law of karma is always operating. To think otherwise would be to assume that karma is stored somewhere in some massive bookkeeping system and then at some specific time, the debt is paid. Each person possesses the light of Christ, the genius of Buddha, the insight of Mohammed, the greatness of every being in and out of incarnation. The Second Coming, like the Day of Judgement, occurs on the day that we recognize our divine heritage and utilize it for good. One client, speaking as his Greater Self, stated it this way:

> *With each thought you think, with each breath you breathe, with each step you take, you sit in judgement on yourself, and without the benefits of jury, you decide whether you are in step with the universe or out of step. You know by your feelings each moment that you breathe where you stand, and you either ignore the feelings or you make some adjustments. There is no final decision, for the consequences would be too great.*

10. *You seem to be anti-religion in some of your views.*

My philosophy, which is not unique by any means, attempts to explain, not undermine. Remember that the substance of this book has evolved over years of working with many, many people of diverse religious backgrounds. They have represented virtually every known religious and personal philosophy. Yet there is predictable consistency in their hypnotic responses to the issues presented in this book.

11. *There is a lot of talk lately about test tube babies and cloning. How do these new methods affect the idea of unique Souls?*

Looking at the issue from a higher perspective than the emotional, one can see that the universe does not differentiate between a womb and a test tube or an incubator. All are places of growth where nutrients are provided so that a new Soul-vehicle is produced. A certain Soul may be looking for the challenge of a body with this early developmental environment. We are not dealing with a question of morality, as far as the universe is concerned, but with an issue of safety and feasibility for the people involved. A greater issue for the new infant comes after birth when the Soul becomes fully focused in the new body and the need for love and attention is unrealistically strong. Incubator babies are prone to feel unloved and ignored, creating great anxieties in adult years. The artificial environment triggers old rejections of past lives. Love must be given in abundance whether the child grows in a womb or in a glass case.

12. *Several psychics have told me about my own past lives. Can these be accurate or is it a hoax?*

It certainly depends on the sincerity and sensitivity of the person to whom you have turned for information. Informal experiments that I have conducted have validated the past-life impressions of several psychics in the San Francisco area. To preclude any carry-over into the regression, the regression comes before the past-life reading. Without giving any clues to the past-life reader, the client must be in as neutral a space as possible, trying not to think of the regression experience. In numerous cases, including one experience of my own, the reader has accurately described the past-life or lives. The most impressive experience to date was the case of the young housewife who experienced eight past lives in hypnosis and then was told about six of them by a noted psychic.

13. *You seem to place great emphasis on past lives as the place where traumas first occurred, yet I can remember nearly drowning as a child and I am afraid of water now. Certainly many problems come from childhood.*

All traumas are learned, so they have to begin somewhere with some incident. You experienced a frightening incident with water that created what could be a longterm fear memory. It is important that it be resolved before you end this lifetime or you surely will carry it into your next lives, creating problems in each of them. Most of us experience frightening moments in the water as children, and yet have no fear of water as adults. It seems likely that the fear of water becomes a serious problem only for those who drowned in a past life. Regressions have borne this out. Debilitating fears are usually based on more than just close calls in this lifetime.

14. *Do you think there is any validity to the idea that people in mental institutions are merely struggling with past and future lives?*

Like all generalizations, this is partly right and partly wrong. Certainly many multiple personalities (such as Eve in *Three Faces of Eve*) and countless institutionalized individuals are unable to control the intrusion of past and future selves, but there are many imperfectly defined phenomena occurring with people who are unable to describe their problem. Most institutionalized people are resistant to hypnotic regression, so there is no way of being sure whether the past is intruding or whether a fantasy is being created. Time seems to be irrelevant to the multiple personality, with yesterday overlapping today and tomorrow. Images overlap as well, and seem to prevent any personal privacy; the person feels as though he or she is a receiver for several stations broadcast simultaneously.

Jan Erenwald, M.D., world renowned psychiatrist and author, feels that some forms of mental illness represent a weakening of the control valves of the brain, so that the individual is overwhelmed with psychic information. Carl Jung took a slightly different view when he stated the neuroses represent an alienation from instincts – facets of consciousness splitting off from instinctual aspects of the psyche.

15. *You have said that the universe manifests everything literally. Exactly what do you mean by that?*

Our emotions, no matter what they are, carry strong messages to the all-encompassing energy system we call the universe. The universe does not judge what is good or bad for us. It interprets all emotional signals as needs, so it responds to all signals with equal intensity. If we think and feel hate, the universe produces something for us to hate. If we feel fear on a regular basis, the message to the universe is clear: manifest something for me to fear and keep producing it until I am satisfied.

Of course, we do not consciously want negatives in our lives, yet we persist in sending our negative emotional signals that can be interpreted only one way. Equally strong and obvious, are the love signals and joy vibrations, and like the negative, we produce these too. We are given people and things to love and enjoy.

Our words are often clear indicators of the kind of emotional signals we are broadcasting to the universe. A good example recently came from a client who learned this concept the hard way.

> This thing hit home with me when my nose was broken: I was bleeding; my face was a disaster area. They stole my wallet. I had just started a new job and really was putting a lot of energy into it. I kept saying and thinking that I didn't want to be bothered with Christmas. I remember saying to many people, 'I don't want to face it this year'. Well, I didn't have to face it – literally. My face was a mess. My eyes were so swollen I could hardly see. The universe took me at my word, but I'm glad I learned it early, because otherwise I may have gotten more messed up with it after that. It was a tough lesson to learn, but now I watch what I say and feel, because I don't want some things to happen as I say them. They're just figures of speech.

16. *In a number of cases, you indicate that the person who came for counselling was relieved of the problem after one session. That sounds too contrived to me.*

As contrived as it may seem, it is true that some people solve their problems in one session. Re-experiencing the events of the past just once can relieve blocks to living. However, most people need a series of sessions to accomplish this.

17. *Your view of death seems cold and unfeeling. You seem to view it in terms of machines being destroyed, rather than people dying.*

I would call the view realistic rather than unfeeling. We have become so used to a ritualized pattern of feelings over death that most of us don't know how we really feel about the subject until we stand back and take an objective look. To get at the truth, we must always be detached enough to see clearly. We often let our emotions and the responses of others dictate what we feel, or what is right and acceptable. Certainly, we feel sadness when a loved one crosses over, but the sadness for the loss of physical presence then needs to be replaced by the knowledge of continuing contact and mutual growth on two different levels of perception. Taking the emotionalism out of death leaves us with a very different picture from the one we may have been taught as a child.

18. *Some people believe that humans can return as animals or – worse yet – insects, if we do wrong in this lifetime. Is this possible?*

No more so than it is possible for a lemon tree to produce watermelons. Animals and humans, like lemons and watermelons, belong to the same classification, but each has distinctive vibrational patterns. This difference in energy patterns prevents interbreeding. Humans always return as humans, period.

19. *How do you account for the increasing world population if the same souls are going out of and coming into incarnations all the time?*

We assume that world population is at its highest today because it has been increasing during the past two hundred years or so. Actually we have no idea what the population of the earth was ten thousand years ago – or even a thousand years ago, for that matter. It could easily have been greater than it is today. If we subscribe to the belief in the ancient civilization of Atlantis, which perhaps existed millions of years ago, we must give some credence to the population figures that emerge from regressions to that time. Numerous clients have mentioned overcrowding, cities running into cities, measures to control population, and emigration to distant lands to relieve the pressures of the masses. Population figures in the billions have often been cited for Atlantis.

Nothing says that souls are limited to existences on this planet, either. Some people have regressed to lives on other planets, while Greater Selves have made a point of talking about the entire universe as the home of Souls. We must keep in mind, too, the theory that Souls reincarnate in cycles that last from one or two generations to hundreds of years. We could now be in one of the high population periods but headed into a decline.

20. *What is the best indicator of the person who is truly spiritual?*

Since spirituality, creativity, and maturity are all interwoven, it is difficult to comment only on spirituality. Let's look at the issue from the person's place of growth. The strongest indication of a person's place of growth would be the degree to which he or she rejects retaliation as a mode of behaviour, especially when the intent to injure is obvious. The best examples of this occur at the most mundane levels of human interaction every day, when someone cuts ahead in a line, for example, or a friend ignores your greeting, or misses a birthday, or make some disparaging remark about your new coat. It's ignoring the attack on the ego without any reprisal thoughts that separates the advanced person from the one who is moving at a slower rate or has had fewer earthly growth opportunities. The advanced soul deals creatively with all situations, especially those that trigger others. There is a direct and assertive action without any reaction.

21. *I have heard that a unique aspect of your regression work involves dealing directly with a past self. Can you explain that?*

For a small percentage of clients, contacting the Greater Self affords access to troubled selves of the past. By way of the usual hypnosis process, the client is able to step aside mentally and allow a personality of the past to enter the counselling situation, so that the client is no longer in the chair before me, but the past self is there instead. The counselling process is directed at the past self, not at the present being who is removed from the counselling environment. At this Level Five state, facial features change, and usually speech patterns and word choice show noticeable differences. As the past self experiences its trials and traumas in a setting of acceptance and understanding, the present self senses a relief, a freeing of the distracting past self. Accomplishing such a feat is gratifying for the counsellor as well as for the client, for it is a direct and complete release of portions of the Self that have been unwilling to learn on a higher level of awareness. These past energies have clung tenaciously to the misconceptions and the pains of the earth plane until confronted in a modern counselling situation and forced to move into the next level of growth experience. Dealing with past selves so directly is not all that surprising to some members of the scientific community. Harold Puthoff and Russell Targ, for example, in their fine book *Mind Reach: Scientists Look at Psychic Ability* state:

> *Although information is usually observed to travel from the present to the future, we should not be upset if experiments are devised that show that sometimes information is found to be transmitted in the other direction. Indeed, the equations of psychics contain discarded solutions which correspond to just this case. This suggests models which may begin to provide a working description of precognition*
>
> . . .

22. *How is deja vu connected to past or future lives or to Greater Self awareness?*

Déjà vu, meaning *already seen,* is the strange sense of knowingness that we experience in a situation, so that we feel we have known about a portion of the situation ahead of time. It is like a replay that is familiar and yet not totally predictable. Almost any situation can spark *déjà vu,* and when it is happening we feel a lightness and a slight separation from what is happening around us.

Through precognition or clairvoyance we seem to be able to 'tune into' a situation before we are involved in it. We forget the rules about time and glimpse the future. This glimpse can occur in a dream or in wakefulness, but it occurs at such deep levels of consciousness that we are not aware of it as it happens. It might be compared to seeing one or two frames of a film before seeing the entire film and then registering some familiarity as the previewed frames are shown along with all the other frames. This common occurrence tells us that we can see the future and controlling this seemingly haphazard event could open doors of awareness that would help us plan more effectively for the future.

23. *How do organ transplants affect the total self?*

There is no effect on the total self, any more than the self is affected by the death of cells in the body that occur by the millions every day, except for the stresses that may be created by such severe operations.

24. *What are the ten most absurd explanations for reincarnation you have heard?*

People who claim to have experienced past lives

1. are really making it all up for attention and/or publicity.
2. are frustrated actors and actresses.
3. are really just remembering movies and books of childhood.
4. are indulging in fantasy and nothing more.

5. are weak-minded or suffering from some mental illness.

6. are really recalling family memories passed on by the DNA molecule that we inherit.

7. are in telepathic contact with the hypnotist who is feeding the information by thoughts.

8. are using psychometry, touching something of a dead person's and knowing about the person.

9. are trying to make their lives more exciting and glamorous by experiencing 'past-lives' of fame.

10. are attempting to invalidate Western religion in a conspiracy.

25. What is meant by 'Akashic Records'? I have heard psychics use the phrase.

The Akashic Records might be called the Library of Universal Knowledge. It is commonly believed that all information on any subject is accessible through meditative trance states and that even past-life memories are part of this body of information. Some dispute the fact that past-life memories are truly one's own memories, but are instead a small portion of the Akashic Records. I feel that the Akashic Records amount to the Greater Self, who does not identify itself but applies answers to the issues in question.

26. What are the most frequently raised objections to the theory of reincarnation that you hear and how do you answer them?

1. REINCARNATION IS AN EASTERN IDEA THAT HAS NO PLACE IN THE WESTERN WORLD.

Great minds through the ages have embraced the concept because it has been their own personal conviction, not because they have read about it somewhere. From Plato to Pythagoras, from Bronson Alcott and Alexander the Great to William Butler Yeats and William Wordsworth, men and women of renown have lived and written of their conviction.

2. NO ONE HAS EVER COME BACK TO TELL US WHAT IT WAS LIKE.

    Every day people are clinically dead on operating tables, in car accidents, under frozen lake surfaces, and yet, when revived, recount experiences in the afterworld. These accounts verify the comments made by people in hypnosis recounting past lives and the crossing over state after physical death. The works of Drs Raymond Moody and Elizabeth Kübler-Ross have added much valuable insight into the subject of after-death awareness.

3. MANY SCIENTISTS AND PSYCHOLOGISTS DO NOT ACCEPT THE CONCEPT.

    Accepting a theory that is 'unprovable' and cannot be dissected under strict laboratory conditions is not easy for many people in science. Also it is natural to reject a different point of view, the truth of which could negate long-held lines of thinking.

4. IT'S NOT WHAT I WAS TAUGHT!

    We are not taught many truths because our teachers are not aware of them. The true teacher is the inner one that encourages personal experiences and discourages blind adherence to the words of others.

5. I DON'T FEEL ANY PAST LIVES INFLUENCING ME.

    Then why are you afraid of height, why do you drink so heavily, why are you always angry with everyone, why are you unable to relate to your youngest daughter, why are you a mechanical genius, why can you play the piano without having taken one lesson? Think twice about every strongly positive and negative aspect of your personality and realize that they all come from somewhere. Genetics and environment can explain only a fraction of them.

6. REINCARNATION AND PAST-LIVES RECALL IS A ROMANTIC
NOTION.

If personal responsibility and letting go of victim roles is a
romantic notion, then we had better take a second look at all the
things of life we avoid and reject and perhaps we can label them
as romantic notions as well. The principal concept of reincarnation is karmic responsibility. Certainly this is realism, not roman-
ticism, because it requires total awareness and understanding of
Universal Law. No one walks into the sunset and lives happily
ever after unless this is designed by action in preceding days,
weeks, months, years, lives.

27. *What is the strangest experience you have had in conducting regressions?*

There have been many strange and interesting ones, and I'm sure
there will be many more, but one that stands out in my mind
occurred when the wife of a client wanted to observe the regression
of her husband. Since I have never allowed direct observation, even
with client consent, I suggested that she listen in the next room with
the door ajar. About halfway into the regression experience, I heard
from the other room details of a different town in strangely accented
English. Another question produced the same thing: answers came
from two places – the client before me, and his wife in the other
room. Fortunately neither person disturbed the other in this regression that evolved in a most unexpected way. I had a sensitive
recorder operating which recorded both sets of responses, which
I later separated into two distinct regressions.

28. *Do clients ever speak in foreign languages during regressions?*

I have encountered several cases of attempts to speak in foreign
languages. However, my instructions at the beginning of a regression to understand and speak only in English unless directed otherwise, keeps the communication in English. Several times, clients
have spoken expressions of their past-life language and uttered

expressions upon request. These examples have ranged in quality from greatly distorted to flawless. Of course, the only cases even worth mentioning are those in which the person in this life has not had any education in the foreign language.

29. *Does a second regression, separated from the first by several months or years, produce some repeating of earlier information?*

Even sessions ten years apart (this is the longest separation I have personally conducted) produce identical facts, but always expand on information given in the earlier session. One client experienced one session a year for six years and in five of those sessions the same past life came to the surface, always mentioning earlier facts and adding new material. The total represents an autobiography of sorts.

30. *If we have lived so many lives, why are we not much further advanced?*

We erroneously equate reincarnation with progress. Reincarnation only provides the opportunity for progress, not a guarantee. Following this false reasoning by comparing lives to days, then someone who is forty would be at least twice as wise as someone who is twenty, and senior citizens would be sages.

31. *What will make the greatest difference in the direction mankind is headed? What will turn us around to live in peace?*

Man's greatest advancement will occur when he (individually and collectively) discovers the difference between instinct and intuition, when he stops talking and starts listening, when he begins responding creatively and stops reacting instinctively.

32. *What would you say would be the biggest step each of us could take to transform the past and set the stage for a positive future?*

Love more, fear less.

19

LIVING IN THE NOW

Trust no future, howe'er pleasant!
Let the dead Past bury its dead!
Act – act in the living present!
Heart within, and God o'erhead!

HENRY WADSWORTH LONGFELLOW,
A PSALM OF LIFE

Perhaps the most important reason for exploring past lives in a therapeutic setting is that the process frees us to focus on the Now Moment. Preoccupation at a subconscious level with the traumas of the past is seriously detrimental to our vitality and growth in the present; yet so often we are unaware of our vulnerability to past events and the painful debilitation that we endure. In an age when our full energies and attention are essential, we cannot afford to be distracted by the past or to operate on 'automatic pilot', even for an instant, for we then become susceptible to all negative energies. Ignorance of the forces that shape our lives must be replaced with self-knowledge if we are to be fully responsible beings.

Looking to the past, we realize that it is not the traumatic experience *per se* that is the crippler – it is the continuing emotional reaction to the experience that makes its mark on the mind and becomes the prison to progress. Preventing ourselves from suffering unnecessary pain – both in the future and in the past – requires that we begin today to recognize old programmed reactions before they become fixed in the subconscious and passed on through Soul memory.

In a troublesome situation we must become sensitive to the

impact of the emotions and then take positive and assertive action that reduces the emotional impact. To do this, we must establish *objective awareness* – a non-emotional perspective that connects us with higher dimensions of the self. Automatically, the authority of our primitive emotional system is repudiated as an interpreter of reality. Allowing the Greater Self to provide perspective means that all threats, fears, guilts, and hurts melt like icicles in the sun. We feel calm, in control, and unscathed by the troublesome situation.

One simple question can trigger this objective awareness: 'From what place and time am I experiencing the circumstances around me?' The answer that we understand through intuitive insight, thought-forms, or actual words heard in the mind is often 'the past'. If we are reliving situations from a past time and place, we can consciously choose to move ahead to the Now Moment. Putting ourselves into proper time synchronization and place location sometimes requires the help of a skilled professional, but there is much that can be accomplished in working with one's self through recognition of the triggering mechanisms of daily life. Assessing life in this way leads us to vigilance towards those people, places, and events that carry us back to past hurts.

Gaining objective awareness in all situations is the technique most easily acquired by anyone who really wishes to change the quality of life in a personal and in a general sense. There are other techniques as well. Most of these require the active process of changing negative thoughts and emotions into positive ones. Everyone at one time or another has heard the expression 'Look at the bright side'. This, of course, is the essence of the idea, but an oversimplification of the concept. To bring light into darkness, to dispel the icy grip of fear, to alter the course of resentment and frustration, we need to understand and practise loving.

Love is our most direct path to emotional and spiritual freedom. By loving more, we cancel the past and communicate directly with the present. This kind of love *must* be unconditional, which means that it must be patient, releasing, and free of all expectations. There is nothing emotional about unconditional love. So often we focus all our love on a select few, then become jealous and possessive when our survival seems to depend on them. We need to love more freely beyond the limits of personal concerns about gain and loss, trusting that the energies that we send out will return to us abundantly.

As we experience the abundance of love that is available to us from Divine Mind, from the Universe, we are able to release obsessions with what others may think of us, as well as our drives to find solace in material possessions. We have always known, at some level, that material things can never sufficiently fulfill our needs in everyday life. We know that our deepest needs are for love and for meaning, for truth and light, and when we shift our gaze from the material and the emotional, we find poetry, music, scripture, art, and dance, the real Soul-pleasers because they lead us from the petty to the purposeful, from the insignificant to the inspirational.

Living in the Now with full responsibility for our sense of loving is not easy, but it is simple. In fact we can reduce all the directives for successful living into an easily remembered ABC formula:

A . . . Act, do not react, in *all* situations.
B . . . Be in the Now, believing in your Self.
C . . . Confront all situations through direct communication.

Responding directly to situations rather than taking the detour of avoidance, inaction, or emotional attack takes faith and flexibility as well as persistence and patience. Expectations of others must be replaced by goals for the Self. Criticisms and judgements must be replaced by patient indifference to the actions of others.

ACTING VERSUS REACTING

The need for attention, recognition, approval preoccupies so much of our time that it is no wonder we are exhausted before we expend physical energies. We think we must show our strength by lashing out at others or at ourselves. The small ego-self does not like to feel small. It does not ever wish to be reminded of what it really is: a false preceptor of daily reality. So it has the 'natural' tendency to strike out at any threat from any direction. It may be the neighbour who fails to say hello; it may be the car that refuses to start; it may be the traffic during rush hour. It can be any person, place, circumstance, or thing, even a thought in one's own mind that can trigger a past hurt and cause a lashing out. Reactions are destructive to the self and to the object of the reaction. Nothing is solved. Instead, we imprint the hurt on our emotional self and intensify feelings of insecurity, helplessness and powerlessness.

Rising above the circumstances of life and loving them as stepping stones to insight, allows us to respond; to act, rather than react. A threat is not a threat if we are bigger than it is. With all old threats, we must grow in our image of ourselves, and in the eyes of the Universe, we do grow, negating the traumas of past lives. It is important for us to realize that people are human. Like us they are depending upon their senses, their egos, as indicators of reality. We must not accept their feelings of insecurity and fear as our own, or intensify theirs by reacting. If we are truly objective, we realize that we have set ourselves up, unintentionally for the most part, but we have placed ourselves in situations where our response is tested.

BEING IN THE NOW, BELIEVING IN SELF

We cannot hope to believe in ourselves if we are dwelling in the past or worried about the future. Such placements of our energies robs us of power and leaves us defenceless in the present moment. And certainly believing in self is a most difficult task in these troubled times when feelings of helplessness and impotence abound. Such feelings stem, not from spiritual lack, but from disappointments related to the physical world and our difficulty in stopping the flow of old feelings. Belief in self grows as one turns inward and contacts that encouraging, loving, all-abiding Greater Self that never fails to provide the guidance needed to solve the problems and challenges of all realities. We must remind ourselves daily that we are *not* the chequebook that fails to balance, nor the fretful person ahead of us in the grocery line, nor the relative that will not understand our position. Each of us is a unique Soul with mind, body, intuitions, and emotions, and sometimes we have difficulty coordinating all these components to produce our desired results. But as long as we realize our spiritual source, we can never be alienated from ourselves and from truth for very long. If we tell ourselves daily that we are spiritual powerhouses of insight and loving patience and then manifest these awarenesses in our daily actions, we cannot help being directed, happy, and purposeful beings. The past has no power over us – nor do the triggering mechanisms of the present – when we are believing that we are more than the fearful thoughts of the ego self.

CONFRONTATION THROUGH COMMUNICATION

Some people associate confrontation with anger and aggressive assault. Confrontation, in a very real sense, dispels the anger before it precipitates assault in an emotional or physical sense. Confronting all situations through effective communication is not easy when feelings of powerlessness are deep, but it is possible if we remember that communication occurs on all levels of self at all times. Verbal communication carries only a small portion of the message we wish to convey. We speak with our bodies, with our eyes, with our minds, with our hearts, with our energies, with our Souls.

Avoiding situations or people, hoping that they will disappear and the problem will solve itself, is an avoidance of living in the Now as well as an avoidance of problem-solving through communication. Even if the confrontation is uncomfortable for the moment, it is necessary to prevent shock waves extending back to the past and ahead into the future. We must be direct in our communications if we wish to love ourselves and to understand others more completely. When we avoid knowing, we misinterpret events and carry unresolved energies into all phases of Life. We can call upon our spiritual essence to support us in times of emotional crisis, when faltering and cowering in the dark corners of life, but we need not wait until ineffective communication forces us into these corners of emotional and physical stress. Our Soul wants to help, to be communicated with, to be instrumental in all the directions we take on a daily basis.

In the entire history of humankind, no subject has been more controversial or inspired more philosophy, art, and human exploration than the question of the existence and nature of the human Soul. It is doubtful whether everyone will soon be convinced that consciousness survives physical death; but each of us must discover, for ourselves, the truth of this universal law.

Even when belief systems have outlived, and have invalidated, themselves through ambiguities and conflicting premises, they persist because they are identified with basic security by so many. Reincarnation is an old truth, perhaps as old as man, and yet it is forever new and exciting. Even for those who cannot consciously view themselves as representatives of the grand plan of the universe, this most basic truth – that humans are immortal – is recognized as some deeper level.

As we grow beyond the need for dogmatic belief systems predicated on rights and wrongs, shoulds and should nots, we turn to explore the realities within. To survive the hard exigencies of each succeeding age, we *must* turn inward and recognize the spiritual energy that stimulates creativity and excites the will. More and more we need a focus that helps us to understand our immortality experientially, and to express it in terms of personal responsibility for the quality of life on all levels. We require a new direction that can elicit the primal genius of each unique Soul and, in turn, awaken a sleeping civilization.

As we turn within ourselves for answers, for peace, for purpose, so we move outside ourselves into the cosmos. Territorialism diminishes, and each person's desperate plea for recognition and approval is quieted by universal acceptance. Each disappointed heart is healed by visions that extend beyond personal pain.

Never forget that imagination, not intellect, guides the questioning mind to truth. Intuition, not instinct, sets us free. One person's Greater Self spoke these words for all of us:

With every sunset, with every rainbow, with every unique snowflake that falls upon the surface of your land, there is beauty beyond compare in all the universe. Let your visions of hope begin with these works of art that are so accessible to you, and then move out and beyond every limitation you thought was in your way. You can love far more than you ever thought possible. Begin erasing the past today by loving more and more with each tomorrow.

Could we but see the pattern of our days
We should discern how devious were the ways
by which we came to this, the present time,
This place in life
And we should see the climb our soul has made
Up through the years.
We should forget the hurt,
The wanderings, the fears, the
Wastelands of our life
And know that we could come no other way
Or grow into our good without these steps our feet have trod
Our faith found hard to meet.
The road of life winds on, and we like travellers
Go from turn to turn until we come to know the truth
That life is endless, and that we, forever,
Are inhabitants of all eternity.

MARTHA SMOCK, *NO OTHER WAY*
UNITY SCHOOL OF CHRISTIANITY

INDEX

The Alternative Therapies Council can be contacted at:
P.O. Box 3415 Stateline Sta., Nevada 89449, USA.